LIMITED EDITION

#63

"LIFE IS AN INCURABLE DISEASE"

ABRAHAM COWLEY

Theres a lot of ghost stories about this place, a lot of rumors of it being haunted, but more importantly it's like the place is haunting. Like for some reason the history is just wanting to be told.

1928, Kentucky, a horrific disease known as 'The White Plague claimed over thousands of lives.

A monstrous Sanatorium was built to isolate and play host to bizarre experiments in desperation to find a cure.

Unable to cope with the large amount of corpses, a Five hundred foot underground body chute was constructed for the removal of these bodies, hiding the enormous death toll from the rest of the outside world. This was called "The Death Tunnel.

*A cure was found and the hospital closed down. This 800,000 square foot monument to pain and suffering lay empty and dormant...*UNTIL NOW!

SPOOKED TV BOOK SERIES

presents

THE

INCURABLE

HISTORY AND HAUNTING OF
WAVERLY HILLS SANATORIUM

BASED ON SPOOKED THE GHOSTS OF
WAVERLY HILLS SANATORIUM
AS SEEN ON SYFY

Volume One

THE INCURABLE

The History and Haunting of Waverly Hills Sanatorium

©2016 By Christopher Saint Booth

SPOOKED TV BOOK SERIES V.1

ISBN-13: 978-0692720790
ISBN-10: 0692720790

SPOOKED TV PUBLICATIONS

18017 CHATSWORTH STREET #130

GRANADA HILLS, CALIFORNIA, 91344 USA

Email: info@spookedproductions.com

Phone: 310-498-9576

www.spookedtv.com

Back Cover Photography from SPOOKED

by Philip Adrain Booth and Robert Correa

and Christopher Saint Booth

©2005 Spooked Productions

Art Design by Christopher Saint Booth

©2016 Christopher Saint Booth

TABLE OF CONTENTS

INTRODUCTION

The phone rang on what seemed to be another sunny day in the town that never rains. More than routine was on the Hollywood agenda. A producer I had previously worked with was on the phone pitching his new movie idea. The films synopsis was a story about cat burglars breaking into an art exhibit for a heist of the century. The location he wanted to use was an abandoned sanatorium in Kentucky. Apparently he and his brother used to break into it when they were kids. It was his mission to have Philip (my brother) and I go down there, write the script and make a movie. First rule of Independent filmmaking is to write your script around the location. So off I went, googling away to find out everything I could about this strange location so we could adapt it into the script. After searching on the Internet for days, I found a wealth of knowledge about this abandoned structure in Kentucky. It was called Waverly Hills Sanatorium and it had nothing to do with cat burglars, art exhibits or a heist of the century.

Research is everything when it comes to documenting the truth, especially when it comes to create entertaining projects that use marketing gimmicks such as "based on true events." Little did I know that what I was researching would not only be a huge turning point in my career but would also change my life. It was intriguing and yet scary as hell, for there is nothing scarier than the truth.

Waverly Hills Sanatorium was a place for hope and chances. But it was also a sad, desolate place filled with oppression and death for the many TB patients who did not find a cure. TB (short for tubercle bacillus) is known as Tuberculosis that is a disease caused by a bacterium called Mycobacterium - Tuberculosis. The bacteria usually attacks the lungs, but TB bacteria can attack any part of the body such as the kidneys, spine, and brain. If not treated properly, TB disease can be fatal.

Tuberculosis was once the leading cause of death in the United States. It was also known as the White Death and the White Plague. What seems barbaric today was a common practice back then as many torturous operations were performed.

This Sanatorium held a lot more then just pain as Waverly Hills is known to be one of the most haunted places in the United States if not the world. Plagued with a tragic history and haunting of dead patients still walking the halls today, for many local residents, Waverly Hills was there monster and this is their story.......

MONSTER OF

A BUILDING

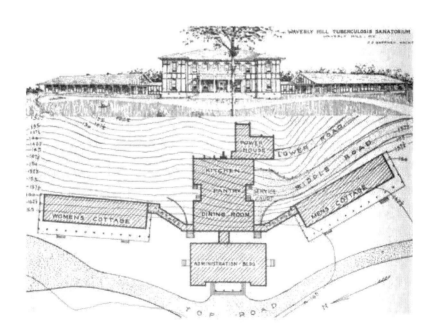

The first time I ever laid eyes on this place when I was a young child around 5 or 6 years old says local Ronald Parkhurst; I would be going down to my grandmother's farm, driving up and down dixie highway. Grandma, what is that? What is that place up there? I would look up and I'd see that tower looming above the trees, she referred to it as a crazy hospital. Don't you ever go up there, I just wondered what in the world lurked in that old building.

A girl describes the Death Tunnel as she could see actual movement and it just got busier and busier, and you could just see shadows passing each other. You see, when that train came by, all these bodies from Waverly had to be disposed of so they had to come, the train had to come here.

She encountered what she said was a girl, a girl that was, umm, not normal. Her brother kept saying she had no eyes. It really freaked him out and he said he would never come back up to this building again.

If you look up at the top of the building where the bell towers are, lots of times you'll see the windows go dark like a figure or someone's walking across in front of the window.

Ex-resident security guard John Harr screams: "If it's gonna get ya, It's gonna get ya. Nobody's gonna save ya, no gun, no knife, no fist. Nothing. It's gonna get ya."

Five steps in you feel swallowed. You hear all kinds of noises, you see all kinds of things. There are lights seen in the building when there is no electricity. Shadows moving around, disembodied voices and apparitions. I wanted to find out the truth of what scared the local folks about this haunted abandoned Tuberculous hospital, like you would even need more than that.

"What does Waverly Hills mean to you when you first hear it?"

One local girl said and I quote,

"I don't know I just know it's scary, scary as hell."

But before we get to the spooky part lets learn about the history of Waverly Hills Sanatorium.

A long time ago in 1908 they decided to build this hospital, they were looking for a place that was way out from the city. At one time Jefferson County was way out in the middle of nowhere as Kentucky had one of the highest Tuberculosis death rates in the US. They found this place on top of this hill that had a breeze most of the time, and that's where they decided to build a hospital. They started by building a small wooden one that housed 40 patients and a handful of doctors.

Medical directors were Dr. Forster 1908-1910, Dr. Dunning S. Wilson 1910-1917, Dr. John B. Floyd 1917-1918, Dr. Pirkey 1918 and Dr. Oscar Miller 1918-1930.

The hospital was indeed small and overcrowded. The patients and staff had most of what they needed to survive when living in the sanatorium. Food was kept in the downstairs dry storerooms. Meals were served in the cafeteria of potatoes, green vegetables and livestock, mostly hogs and chickens raised on the property. As it was an embarrassment for patients to go in to town for there needs as many of the townsfolk frowned upon theses sick individuals and treated them as poor leapers.

Due to the Kentucky flood in May of 1927, or so the officials say, all of Waverly's records, files has been either lost or destroyed. What is apparent is, if you one of the unlucky to contract the TB disease, recovery was slim to none, basically you received your death sentence. Driving up to Waverly was likely the last place you would ever see. It was a sad and desperate time with one hope, that you would not get the rest of your family infected as they would surely suffer the white death. All hoped for a cure for the incurable.

When the numbers of infected got out of hand, thanks to the Anti-Tuberculosis Association, made up of the city's elite and wealthy, they helped create awareness and utter-panic to help raise money from the state to build a new larger hospital of 800,000 square feet. Dr. Oscar Miller was in charge of the move.

Completely fireproof, being made mainly of concrete and marble, It was completed in 1926. It had a completion price of 1.1 million dollars back in 1926. So this was a very large expenditure at that time. Because Tuberculosis, the *White Plague*, was really wreaking havoc on the public, a lot of people were dying. As the epidemic grew so did the sanatorium.

The back of the building had a curvature (bat-wing design) to it that faces to the south-west. And that's the way that the general breeze blows all the time, year-round. The building was designed this way with a curvature to the back so it would capture the wind and try to create a breeze that would go through the building all the time, year round.

The hospital has 4 floors and a partial 5th floor. And the first floor was more or less set up with the x-rays and the administration and the gift shops, the library... stuff like that.

When you got to the second and third floor, that was for the general population. Where they stuck as many people in here as they could fit in. And then when you got to the fourth floor, that was for the people that had the money, and if you go to the fourth floor you will notice every room up there has it's own private bathroom. Where on the second and third floor you had a community bathroom, and three or four different places down the hall.

Waverly Hills patient Delores Webster remembers: Well, you know, I was pretty ill at first they thought I had pneumonia, and then they got to doing examinations and said well, it's too late for that, you're a pretty sick girl. So they sent me to Waverly.

Hundreds Arrive In Hope Of Miracle Cure!

Tina Mattingly owner of Waverly Hills Sanatorium explains: There were people who came from all over the world to come here because it was supposed to have been, you know, elite. Top of the line hospital as far as Tuberculosis. There were a lot of locals that weren't able to come and stay here because it had other people from other states here and so they stopped that. You had to be a resident of Jefferson County to be a patient at Waverly Hills.

Delores Webster: They sent me to Waverly and I had just turned seventeen years old so that was a big blow.

This place served as a Tuberculosis Hospital from October 17th of 1926 up until 1961. After that point it closed down for approximately two years and remodeled and reopened as Woodhaven Geriatrics Center which is basically a nursing home, and it remained that until 1980 when it closed it's doors for good.

Patient Delores Webster underlines the scare factor: I did think about it, they used to roll us out onto the porch as they called it, you know the screened in area, and it was really quiet at night and you know we are really kind of helpless lying here, but it never entered my mind to ever be afraid.

Meanwhile Keith Age the resident ghost hunter of Waverly Hills is preparing an investigation of an (after) lifetime.

Waverly Hills Sanatorium has a total of five floors with 435 rooms. Each floor had two nurse's stations except for the fifth floor. The first floor had the X-ray room, morgue, the laboratories and was mostly full of offices and stores such as a barber, beauty salon and even a dentist. They did not want anyone going to town and possibly spreading this disease. At at the peak of the TB epidemic, an average of six deaths were every hour.

Main dining room and cafeteria including a small bakery was on the second floor which could hold up to almost 500 people with a ventilation system that could change the air temperature every 3 minutes.

The average consumption in one meal was 140 pounds of bacon, 100 dozen eggs, 30 pounds of cottage cheese, 30 gallons of ice cream, 9 gallons of syrup, and 190 pounds of liver. In 1 year, in addition to container milk, 1,147 barrels of bulk milk, 13 tons of sugar, 6 tons of butter, and 52,276 pounds of ground beef. An average of 2,100 meals were served daily.

Third floor consisted of patients rooms with the gruesome operating room still standing on the fourth floor.

It is interesting to note as when we were there exploring the OR we had noticed there are two walls, basically a room built inside a room. We never did find out the reason for this except this double room may have been possibly built to help keep the sound of screaming from echoing through out the hospital.

The fifth floor divided in two parts. It was were they kept the more violent and mental patients as well as one could get access to the roof for sun therapy (the heliotherapy department) known as a solarium. It also had access to the elevator and is believed at one time it was a children's ward.

Waverly Hills had a small basement that at one time gave access to a tunnel as well as crawl spaces throughout. It also sported an erie, creepy room that had small windows and low standing tables. What on earth happened here? Possibly a make shift preparation of the dead before departure down the body chute?

The most infamous is the death tunnel or the body chute. Constructed to transport the deceased to the bottom of the hill. This tunnel is a 500-foot tunnel that would carry the bodies down to the crematorium.

The main building was not the end of the expansion; over

the years many other buildings were constructed according to need and patient volume. A few of the buildings were for hospital use, such as: the small water treatment plant, the heating steam plant and the laundry room. The buildings that were constructed for other uses were the Colored hospital, Men's porch, Children's ward, Nurses dorms, Theatre and recreational hall, Radio station, and nine residences for doctors.

Unfortunately, this was still a time of segregation and they were not allowed to seek treatment in the main building. The construction of this building allowed them the same treatment and comfort. The hospital was built with 100 rooms to accommodate as many colored patients as possible. The colored hospital was built in direct need for colored people who were diagnosed with tuberculosis and needed treatment with an estimated cost of 212,000 dollars.

There was an open air schoolhouse that was opened in 1915 to specifically take care of children that had Tuberculosis. Death certificates that have children that had died of Tuberculosis. The Children's ward was built for the children that would inhabit Waverly so that they would be able to continue their studies during their illness. It was built at an estimated 153,000 dollars.

The Incurable: History and Haunting Of Waverly Hills Sanatorium

As written in the Waverly Bulletin, Dec. 1940.

I do not ask that God should spare
My feet from stony paths,
Not do I pray that He will shield
Me from all the stinging.
Forbid that I should whimpering turn,
When my load seems hard to bear.
No, God, I only pray for strength
To be the victor with my share.

When, should I ever think or feel,
That what He bids me to do
Is much too great a task for me –
That I cannot win through?
I'll pray, dear Lord, that Thou wilt open
These blind eyes of mine,
That I might better see and know
This is Thy will divine.

-Kathleen Crawford
Fifth floor, west.

THE FIRST FLOOR

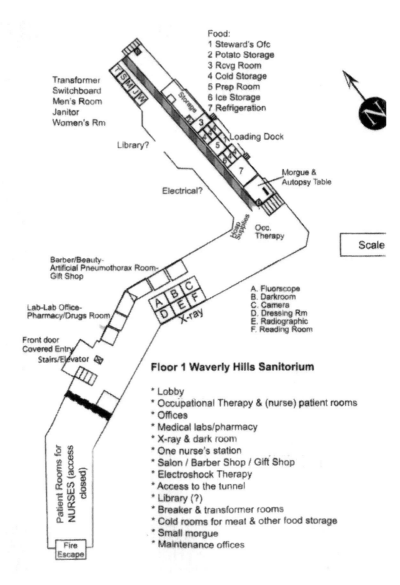

Food:
1 Steward's Ofc
2 Potato Storage
3 Rcvg Room
4 Cold Storage
5 Prep Room
6 Ice Storage
7 Refrigeration

Transformer
Switchboard
Men's Room
Janitor
Women's Rm

Storage

Loading Dock

Library?

Morgue &
Autopsy Table

Electrical?

Occ.
Therapy

Scale

Barber/Beauty-
Artificial Pneumothorax Room-
Gift Shop

A. Fluorscope
B. Darkroom
C. Camera
D. Dressing Rm
E. Radiographic
F. Reading Room

Lab-Lab Office-
Pharmacy/Drugs Room

X-ray

Front door
Covered Entry
Stairs/Elevator

Floor 1 Waverly Hills Sanitorium

* Lobby
* Occupational Therapy & (nurse) patient rooms
* Offices
* Medical labs/pharmacy
* X-ray & dark room
* One nurse's station
* Salon / Barber Shop / Gift Shop
* Electroshock Therapy
* Access to the tunnel
* Library (?)
* Breaker & transformer rooms
* Cold rooms for meat & other food storage
* Small morgue
* Maintenance offices

Patient Rooms for
NURSES (access
closed)

Fire
Escape

W e're gonna be going on up. Waverly's got five floors to it. We're gonna go up the first floor all the way up to the fifth, try to catch all the hot spots that we find. This building can hurt you so please stay with me asserted the leather clad hunter.

"So, You don't think Waverly Hills is haunted?" I asked.

"Not for a minute" screamed Mary Steele a former patient. Mary and her husband was admitted in Waverly Hills for several years.

Meanwhile back at the ghost hunt with Keith Age: "Right now what I've got with me is an array of different equipment. An EMF meter, Electro Magnetic Field meter, this is the sound it makes, and right now it is going off, BIG TIME!"

PARANORMAL INVESTIGATION BEGINS

EMF ELECTROMAGNETIC FIELD A FORCE GIVEN OFF BY ELECTRIC CHANGES, FOUND IN ANYTHING THAT USES ELECTRICITY. THE HIGHER THE SPIKES IN THE ELECTROMAGNETIC FIELD ARE, THE MORE POTENTIAL THERE IS FOR PARANORMAL ACTIVITY.

EMF?, Electromagnetic Field meter, this reads the natural magnetic fields that are all around us constantly, man-made or natural. If a spirit or ghost is here that is what this thing will react to as we tend to get a lot of EVPs in Waverly Hills Sanatorium.

Keith Age explains: When I took a tour here one night the

first thing I tell people is that you can't smoke in here. Just out of respect for what the building was. So what we got was right here, as you hear me talking, on this tape, you hear a cigarette lighter clink, and you hear somebody light their cigarette. You hear the lighter clink back, like it shut, and right behind that you hear, "Put that out, put that out."

Jessica Goldman describes her experience while ghost hunting at Waverly: We was standing that way looking down the hallway at shadows and I was standing there and my ear was right by that window there and it sounded like something was behind me to my left and it sounded like it said no or oh or go or something of that nature. And it was like really hoarse but really... it was almost like ..

Out of Breath?

Yeah, pretty much, it was like....
Couldn't breathe? Having a hard time breathing?
Like it was forced...

Keith continues: We have things where people are screaming, you hear where it says TB is no good, or TB is no fun We've got one that says "Dad Mother please help me," "Someone save me," it's a lot of these mournful, sorrowful cries. We don't know why, other than, we know a lot of people died here.

Some say over 63,000!

EVP ELECTRONIC VOICE PHENOMENA: DISEMBODIED "VOICES" AND SOUNDS
IMPRINTED ON AUDIO RECORDING DEVICES.

Some other Class A EVP's we captured are,

"HOW YOU'RE DOING?"
"I'M THREE YEARS OLD"
"KILL ME"

Waverly historian John Amerine talks of children ghosts:
There was an open air schoolhouse that was opened in 1915 to
specifically take care of children that had Tuberculosis. Death
certificates that have children that had died of Tuberculosis. There
used to be stories of a ghost of a little boy that bounced a ball
around the halls.

"Bobby" is the little boy that is often sighted or heard
playing with an old leather ball. He is known to haunt all of the
floors, using the whole hospital as his playground. He is described
as a young boy in clothes like those of the depression era. His age

is unknown, as his file may have been one of the ones lost in the flood of 1937. It is estimated, though, that his age seemingly is around eight or nine.

Bobby has been sighted several times by many witnesses. On one account, during the haunted house held at Waverly during the month of October, he was viewed standing at a distance, holding his leather ball, watching the crowd curiously. After a while of watching, being a child still regardless of the length of his stay at Waverly, Bobby apparently got bored and disappeared.

He has been spotted leaning against a window ledge on the third floor, as if contemplating. Staring off into the distance, possibly pondering thoughts only a spirit caught in between worlds could ponder. After nearly five to ten minutes of this, he was seen walking away from the window and a faint sound of a ball bouncing was heard.

On another occasion, during another year of the haunted house, Bobby was sighted standing near the entrance to the "death tunnel". Yet again, he had with him his leather ball. When Bobby was approached by the witness, he looked startled, yet surely not as startled as the witness was when the boy then asked, " Why are you here?"

After asking the question in which the witness had no answer, (How do you answer a ghost?) he faded into transparency.

Leaving the viewer speechless and quite flabbergasted.

On the fifth floor/rooftop where the children's swings were located, it is not unheard of to hear the phantom swings as if they too were trapped spirits unable to be released. Perhaps Bobby still swings, to remember a part of living that he may have particularly enjoyed, or possibly to forget his heartache of wandering those halls forever alone.

We asked Delores: "When you were in the Sanatorium did your family take care of your daughter?"

"Yes, they did, They did, my mother did...and it was very hard on her, she took the best care that she could. I don't know where I would have left my baby."

Mr. Thornberry is a long time caretaker of Waverly Hills Sanatorium and at the age of 92 he shares his story:

Now right through here, (pointing at one of the now vacant buildings), like I was telling you, You could come right out that door right there and come in to here. There was a big auditorium with a second floor. And every Wednesday night they'd have picture shows or different entertainment.

Former patient Douglas Steele remembers: "We had entertainment, we had things at Christmas time. Once in a while they had a movie, probably older than the hill, but when you're in there, you enjoy anything."

Mr. Thornberry continues: They'd have a big Christmas party, and out in the front lawn where they'd bring a Santa Clause with reindeers and a sled. He'd unload that sled, that's when I was a child you know and Santa Clause would take them reindeer around for a sleigh ride.

Douglas Steele continues: I just wanted to say something about the good things of Waverly Hills because the people did enjoy themselves to some degree. There was a lot of fun things that went on there. I could tell you some stories that are real interesting. One of the doctors there once had a horse, and he liked to get the patients out and let them ride the horse if they could. He said might as well let them enjoy themselves, because they didn't have as long to enjoy life as some other people did anyway.

"Like a family, Like a family" Mr. Thornberry cries out.

Now lets go inside the hospital, to the first floor.

PARANORMAL INVESTIGATION   167-WHS FIRST FLOOR INVESTIGATION DATA
REASON FOR SUSPECT: UNSETTLED EXCESSIVE DECAY AND SICKLY ODOR
POSSIBLE TARGETS: 8   AVERAGE EMF READINGS: 8 TO 20 M-GAUSS
EVP CHECK DATA.   IRT READINGS-TEMPERATURE: 83   HUMIDITY: 19
COLD SPOTS DETECTED: YES   HOT SPOTS DETECTED: NO
PARANORMAL PHENOMENA: LIKELY   VISUAL PHENOMENA: UNKNOWN

WAVERLY HILLS SANATORIUM, FIRST FLOOR
PARANORMAL PHENOMENA DETECTED, 63 THOUSAND DEAD

Keith Age and I continue on down Waverly's, institutional, oversized halls as Keith describes the surroundings: There was actually a death wing right here. This is where they brought the bodies down. They didn't want the people to see them, we know for a fact that tens of thousands people died here, especially the first year alone when thousands of people died.

They'd bring them in and put them in these freezing chambers but what they realized real soon, really quickly was that they didn't have enough time or space to get all the bodies.

Joe Mattingly a past ex-employee of Waverly Hills admits: They were taking the bodies to the elevator in back and the elevator would break down. All the bodies would be stacked up in front of the elevator...... They had special people to do that....They had a refrigerator and they'd put them in that. That damn freezer at a certain temperature would keep them dead cold.

The first year wave was so heavy, so thick they couldn't get the bodies out of here fast enough.They turned the maintenance room into a makeshift morgue.

Douglas Steele remembers: There was a morgue there, I can remember going in to the morgue where they put bodies, until they could be picked up or autopsied or whatever. And that was right by the back elevator.

With all the deaths in the hospital, a certain percentage of them have to be autopsied. That's a requirement. So they'd end up taking all the bodies down this hallway, down to what is said to be called the draining room.

These questions that we asked Mr. Steele, we were trying to get to the truth.

Theres even more, for this room they called the draining room, It was supposed to be where they hung people, drained their infected blood out of them. It was across from the morgue.

Douglas Steele reacts: There may be something that happened that not everybody knew about. I don't know. I can't comment on it. I don't know about it.

John Amerine jumps in: The Bleeding Room. It's the room on the far end of the kitchen wing, the door just before what is known as the body chute.

Keith Age explains: They would hang the bodies up on these poles and basically slit them from the sternum to the groin and all the way down. Get them out and go to the body chute or the death tunnel.

The original purpose was to be a smoke house, it's where they kept their meat. They were totally isolated up here. They couldn't leave this farm for nothing. But this is where they ended up taking the bodies and hanging them on these hooks and poles and letting the infection drain out as there is a drain over here on the right hand side. At this point they put them back on the gurney, go through the door and take them down to the body chute.

"As far as the draining the body, I've talked to people that were involved in the embalming procedures in the time that Waverly Hills was open and in fact, if anything, they would be worried about letting biohazards loose much less putting it down a drain, sending it down the hill to the sewage system."
-John Amerine, WHS Historian

"They was scared of the sewer and they made a special septic tank of some kind. They claimed it wasn't dangerous the way they had it made." -Joe Mattingly, Former Employee

Tuberculosis-Infection, with or without disease, caused by the bacterium Micro-bacterium tuberculosis.

EDUCATION OF THE PEOPLE AND THROUGH THEM OF THE STATE IS THE FIRST AND GREATEST NEED IN THE PREVENTION OF TUBERCULOSIS.

Weren't you worried about catching the disease yourself? It was very contagious...very contagious I asked Joe, a previous employee of the past Sanatorium.

Joe Mattingly: Yeah, yeah.

So how did you deal with that?

Well, that was another reason I quit.....

You see, they were concerned about carrying disease outside of Waverly Hills. That was a big concern to them. Because they was afraid after going through all this business, of building this place, and then the neighbors would get up a petition and close them down. They done everything they could do says Joe Mattingly.

Charles Mattingly: The community wanted anyone with Tuberculosis to be up here so that they would be quarantined. But I am sure that everybody that came through these doors had hopes of getting better and walking out one day.

Sarah Gilbert/WHS Historian: It was epidemic stage and I guess just knowing how many people lost their lives and how many loved ones had to suffer along with them, and you know there was no cure for TB at the time.

I had asked Doug and Mary Steele, surviving patients of Waverly Hills some personal questions on how they contracted TB.

Douglas Steele: "Yes, My mother. I cared for her for a year or more til she died."

Mary Steele: "I caught mine from my father. Anyhow, I think Daddy got the germ from when he lived with me here in Louisville. He was a vegetable or fruit inspector or something. And he lived with me at that time. I feel like that is when I got it. His germs."

Douglas Steele: "I went to see a specialist in Tuberculosis and he sent me right out there... to Waverly Hills."

"Did they do an Xray, sputum test?"

Mary Steele: "Yeah and it was horrible."

They would lock them away, basically because they didn't know what to do with the disease.

After that they were coming out with antibiotics such as streptomycin and different pills that would cure TB where people could actually just stay home as outpatients.

Mary Steele: "What were those white pills? I don't remember."

Douglas Steele: "Para...Paraminocylic acid."

"There you go."

Douglas Steele: Isolenic... Iso... INH...Isonicotonic hydroxide.   *Whoa! That's a word.*

So people with TB in their skin, of course they would get sunlight and such for treatment, or even artificial UV light.

Douglas Steele: Well, you see, I worked with that at the

29

clinic where we treated patients daily with these lights. They also put them on drugs and they came back regularly to be refilled. If I'd have had some medicine back when it first started out I'd have been in pretty good shape.

"I have brown little Imp looking monster things in all my photographs."

Ex-security guard Roy Muir explains: We actually had a lot of cases where we've done tours in the building, people that don't know each other mentioned the same things, little short little characters that just tend to appear and disappear.

Well I knew it, sounds crazy doesn't it, but if I was you I would start checking your photos, especially the exterior ones, absolutely bloody crazy!!

Cathy Gales was a nurse at Woodhaven and worked there for a year, and in her words *"It was a place where people came to die."*

Below is her written account while at Woodhaven.

I know you may have heard stories of Waverly when it was a nursing home but I want to let you know that this was a very bad place. There were a lot of times I would go to work to find patients laying in a wet bed. Also, they had used the bathroom on themselves and no one had cleaned them up. I also know that there were bugs in the food sometimes. It was a very hot, smelly, sad place to be. The Government paid for most to stay there because they had no family. It was a very sad time. When I first started working there I would cry when I got home because of that place. You always felt the feeling of sadness there. Some people may want to try and make it sound like a good place but I was there and I know it wasn't.

I know the patients I took care of never had anyone come visit unless they came after I was gone which I doubt. Woodhaven was a place that old people would come because nobody else wanted them and they came there to just die. And I think that is very sad. Family should be everything, but these poor people didn't even have that. Now I have worked at a lot of nursing homes but I still have to say Woodhaven was the worst.

I   t was so sad. They had locks on the patients doors so they couldn't get out. They were thin and seemed to never talk. You could look into their eyes and see all the pain and hurt. I took very good care of the patients I had. We were only supposed to give them a bath once a week, but my patients got a bath everyday. I would comb their hair and fix them up to look nice. There was no air conditioning there. There were certain floors we were not allowed to go on. I thought that odd. I put my whole heart and soul into taking care of my patients. But, it is no wonder they shut it down for lack of care. It wasn't supposed to be that way, but it was. We were understaffed, but I did everything I could to make the people there happy.

I remember there was a lady that was a patient I took care of and she never smiled. I tried very hard to make her smile. Then, one day after I gave her a bath and fixed her up all pretty, told her how pretty she looked and gave her a big hug, for the first time since I had been taking care of her, she smiled and hugged me back! That was a wonderful day for me. Then, Three days later, she died. It broke my heart. But, I felt she knew someone loved her.

The whole time I was there, I never saw anyone come and visit any of the patients I took care of. It's sad to think of all they gave to this world and nobody seemed to care. While I was there, most who died, died alone. No family, no friends, no one. Every time I see that building, I felt the sadness and want to cry.

Cathy Gales

Another care-worker from 1976 to 1979 at Woodhaven, Cindy states that the nurses were overworked, causing many of the dire circumstances that lead to Woodhaven's closure.

"Not all patients were unhappy there. I worked the

32

floors helping nurses as an aide the first year I was there and they were certainly overworked. I remember the nurses I was around were not very caring and they treated the patients like you would treat your enemy. The second floor is where they kept the patients who were dying and the one memory of the nurse telling me to "move it" when I stopped to look and see if I could help a lady who was in the hallway on a gurney/bed.

The patient was wailing and moaning since she was tied to her bed she couldn't get up. The nurse who told me to "move it" whispered to me when I caught up to her; that the second floor was for dying patients and not to "even bother with them, they won't be around much longer". That broke my heart and I went down to the volunteer coordinator and switched from working the floors to working in Occupational Therapy.

There were happy patients too. In Occupational Therapy, they had a piano and a very old loom that the women would use. They had patients who snapped green beans and sang their hearts out as other patients played old tunes on the piano. The best experience I had there, I met a blind lady who had been a patient there for three years. I fell instantly in tune with her. When you entered the third floor, you could hear her singing as loud as could be, an old song "The old gray mare she ain't what she used to be" and she would be clapping her hands and smiling even with no one in her room.

You see they had a TB hospital, and then after the TB hospital they had a nursing home. Called it the Woodhaven Geriatrics Center, thats what they called it.

A the nursing home, you had old folks here that passed away from either neglect or abuse or something like that of nature. It was an old peoples type home, where they mistreated everybody. There was urine and cockroaches everywhere.

Nurse Gales shares her pain: When I took care of them, it was like they would be laying in feces, they would be laying in a wet bed, nobody cared about them. There would be times I would sit out in the parking lot and just cry because I didn't want to come in. Because I knew what it was going to be like when I was in here. It was nothing but pure sadness.

People falling off of things because they weren't watched. In their wheelchairs falling off loading docks.

Mr. Thornberry adds: A man in a wheelchair went off that loading dock right there and Killed!

Charles Mattingly co-owner of Waverly Hills Sanatorium explains: This place wasn't kept real well. And the patients weren't taken care of very well.

They tell you to do something, you better do it. Or you was gone says Joe Mattingly.

Nurse Gales continues: They had locks on their doors, and there was once where another nurse was there and she would tie up the patients in their chairs, so I went over there to help her. And the nurse told me to just leave her alone. That she was going to die anyway.

They went crazy, they were naked in cells, they were electrocuting them. Shock therapy. They did a lot of different experiments and such. The state finally closed down Woodhaven in 1982 but by that point it was just complete pandemonium up there.

Writer, Victoria L. Hall currently a hospice nurse today shares her incredible true story "The Brooch!

As a young child I was always eager to help others. While in grade school at St. Paul's on Dixie Highway a group of my friends and I formed a little after school-club. We would make little trinkets and cookies for the sick and shut-in. One fall day we had made arrangements to visit the Old Waverly Hills Sanatorium. During the early 60's the TB hospital had been turned into one of Louisville's first nursing homes. As we entered the massive building we all huddled together. At first it was startling. The air in the building was musky and bursting of stale urine. As we moved along the shadowy and dungeon like corridors crying and ear-piercing moans filled our ears. Unprepared with what we had heard and smelled a couple of the girls ran from the building. Guardedly the last two of us took hands and began to peer over half doors into ominous and dingy rooms. Even at the young age of 11 or so our hearts were touched. To this day I can still conjure up the sounds, sights, and odors of years long ago that I encountered in that building.

Some of the people were lying on beds. Others huddled in corners. Suddenly turning around the other girl had run and I found myself all alone in the shadowy and fear-provoking corridors. As I turned the corner I peered over the half door at a teeny frame of a lady huddled in a corner. She was naked, but quickly moved toward me. Frantically I backed away from the half door. Without any forewarning she reached over the half door grabbing my sweater. The room and halls were cold with a draft that swirled around my legs. I pulled away from her, but not before she grabbed my sweater again. I soon realized that she wanted my sweater and without hesitation I quickly pulled it off handing to the skeleton like figure.

Like a flash she moved across the room grabbing a cardboard box. Opening the box she frantically dug through it searching for something. She stood up and tossed something shiny over the door. Clicking down the hall I couldn't imagine what it might be. Scouring the floor I found a beautiful pearl brooch. I quickly picked it up and laid it back on the half door. Through the whole event the lady never spoke a word, but her piercing green eyes spoke a thousand words to my heart. Several times I placed it back on the half door and repeatedly she tossed it over the door towards me.

I soon understood that it was her gift to me for giving her my sweater. I certainly wanted nothing in exchange for my gift. She would not accept the broach back no matter how many times I put it back on the half door. She simply continued to pick it up and throw it towards me. I remember kissing the brooch in front of her and walking away. My heart had been touched by an act of love and appreciation that to this day some 40 years I have never forgotten. I can still see the microscopic lady huddled in the corner wrapped in my sweater. Over the years I wondered about her. Who she was, did she have family?

I know that from that day forward I was propelled into a destiny of compassion and caring for others in a way that only God could refine over the years as I journeyed through life.

Are you wondering whether I have the brooch today? I don't know how over the many years of moving and growing and life itself, but I do! It's as beautiful today as it was to a young girl of 11years old with wide sparkling eyes as she left such a sorrowful place with her treasure. I wear it often and have had many people comment on it and so it opens a conversation whereby I can share such a cherished experience.

The journey of that day started me on a wonderful nursing career of many years allowing me to cherish and love the suffering and dying in ways I don't think I would have ever been able to do.

Victoria L. Hall

Woodhaven geriatrics hospital was eventually sited and closed down in 1980 due to improper patient care. It was not the first time the hospital was investigated for falsifying patient records saying they were alive knowing that they were really dead just so they could still continue to collect the per-patient funding. Waverly Hills Sanatorium was then left abandoned waiting for its next victims.

MEANWHILE BACK AT THE INVESTIGATION

This is an electroshock therapy room this is the first place we ever broke an EMF meter. The whole time I have being doing this for over 25 years I have never had that happen. There was so much electromagnetic activity in this room it fried the meter. And as you can kinda see from this room it is not very big. They put the patients over there, watched them through a big window. The doctors would stand here and look at this light board here, that would tell them just how much juice was actually going to the board says Keith Age.

John Harr, Waverly local security makes his point: "You know, after seeing stuff I have seen up here, it does let me know that if anybody pisses me off I can come back and haunt the hell out of them."

Ghost hunters come to Waverly and they'll sit up there for hours trying to capture ghosts with their EMF meters and all their electronic gadgets. Most activity that has been captured has been on the third or fourth floor right in the hallway.

What we're looking for is shadows that move. People call them shadow people.

Waverly Hills Sanatorium is notorious for Shadow people.

Here is the typical experience from the local investigators.

So what do you think you exactly saw? Can you describe it?

It was... It was a shadow figure, right beside me.

Shadow Person?

Yeah, it was right beside, I mean like right here beside me.

Waverly co-owner Mr. Mattingly explains: And so, if you hear people that have been in the building they will talk about the shadow people. Where you can actually see them from the outside of the building inside the windows. But sometimes when you are inside the building, you can, especially at nighttime, you can sit and look down the hall and you can actually see a shadow move around in front of you. And you can't explain where it came from.

Tina Mattingly: We think it's trespassers up here and it will walk right in front of us and we light it up with flashlights, and there is nobody there.

Local Investigator Kimberly Johnstone: We were watching the shadow people. They were seeing it for the first time, I was there just kind of as support. And one said don't look to your left, there is one standing right next to you. You could just feel a coldness all down the left side of my body. It was extremely cold and there was no way I was looking to the left side of my body.

Local Investigator Alisha: If you look up there on the second floor you can actually shadows standing there. It looks like people.

Tina Mattingly: And you can go up there any night and there is a break in the light and there is shadows that look like they move towards you..... And you can go up there any night and there is a break in the light and there is shadows that look like they move towards you.

I think we successfully scared the shit out of ourselves.

We're going to try to find a restroom and clean up now.

So if you were to walk past this door you would see a shadow in the hallway. You start seeing one, then you just focus and you start seeing another and another, and it gets faster and faster and it gets closer to you. Shadows of patients walking everywhere, if you look down the hallways, you see like the windows or doorways, and you just see shadows crossing the doors.

Hundreds of shadows, it just gets faster and faster and faster. Just as soon as you're eyes would focus you could see actual movement. And it just got busier and busier and busier. And you could see shadows passing each other, as if there was people walking back and forth.........

We've done tours, where constantly there's shadow people that move throughout the halls, I mean, through doorways, it's kind of like peeking around looking at you. It creeps people out says Roy Muir Waverly security guard.

Waverly security guard Logan spills his beans: I could have swore to God, that I seen this figure turn sideways, and I could see arms and legs, moving down the road and it was moving towards to where I was standing. So I got real Spooked and I thought, you know, I'm not alone, there is somebody trying to sneak up here or sneak back down. So I crept around and tried to get up and try to flank them to where they couldn't see me. I got up to where it looked like it disappeared in the woods and there was nothing there. There was no signs of anybody walking...nothing. And I got on the radio and told everybody that I just chased a shadow person down the road for the first time.

I've seen Shadows that walk outside the building. Shine a light on them, they're not there.

We found out by doing experiments with lasers, these things, it's not cutting right through them. So they do have some type of substance. You can stick a laser light and put it across the shadow and it will stop on the shadow. Cause ghosts have substance.

Keith Age-Ghost Hunter: What's pretty cool is, drop your camera, got your night vision on? Look at that.

Oh my god!

See it moving? Look at that! Look, see it coming closer? Look! See it coming closer? See how close it is? Is that cool or what?   *Ok, Jesus.*

Keith Age: Look at that... I mean, I'm hitting something here. Right here.

Chasing Ghosts, that's what we're doing...

Alisha: Chasing Ghosts...

42

It's getting really cold.

Logan: I can't deal with it. I can't be in the building by myself, I can't walk around by myself. You just get that sick feeling in your body when you're by yourself that is something you don't want to bear.

Alisha: The only people that's ever gotten injured up here is Keith and Jay, through the Louisville Ghost Hunters. They have had drywall thrown at them, They've had bricks thrown at them.

Keith Age: If you hear things whizzing through the air, duck. For the simple fact that it is concrete. Waverly is made out of concrete, not plaster, the walls are concrete. And yeah, I have been on the receiving end a few times and it does not feel good.

In the spiritual world, it's smart and picks up on that, and will not tolerate any negativity crossing their path.

Alisha: Something standing in front of her face, she couldn't see nothing but black and she actually peed on herself.

Tina Mattingly: Cause you never know if it is someone or something.

THE SECOND FLOOR

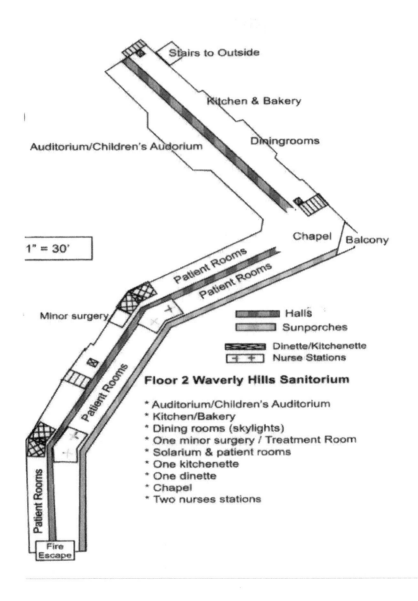

Stairs to Outside

Kitchen & Bakery

Auditorium/Children's Audorium

Diningrooms

Chapel / Balcony

1" = 30'

Patient Rooms

Patient Rooms

Minor surgery

Halls
Sunporches
Dinette/Kitchenette
Nurse Stations

Floor 2 Waverly Hills Sanitorium

Patient Rooms

* Auditorium/Children's Auditorium
* Kitchen/Bakery
* Dining rooms (skylights)
* One minor surgery / Treatment Room
* Solarium & patient rooms
* One kitchenette
* One dinette
* Chapel
* Two nurses stations

Patient Rooms

Fire
Escape

I went up to the second floor one night, at night, I am not sure what time it was, you know the wee hours of the night, and went up with a group of people and it was my first time up there and I was seeing shadows and big white things.

Yeah, Ok, I am getting the fuck out of here..Holy Shit!

Coming towards us. Kinda bouncing around, and we all saw the same thing. There was no reflection or anything it was just like this weird ball of light.

Tom Swartz was a volunteer guard at Waverly Hills and he couldn't wait to tell his story: This is an orb that I photographed on Waverly Hills rooftop in June of 2002. Notice the size of it, notice the concentric rings, notice the eyeball in the middle. I call it the eye orb, but I changed from the eye orb to my companion orb, and I will show you why. In the next photograph you will see the orb, but in my apartment at home. See the rings, see the circle. This orb appeared after I said, Mary Lee, if you would like to be in the picture in my apartment may I take your photograph, thank you. I took the photograph and this orb appeared.

ORB SPHERICAL IMAGE, USUALLY TRANSLUCENT WHITE THOUGH SOMETIMES OF A REDDISH OR BLUISH HUE, WHICH INEXPLICABLY REGISTERS ON FILM AND VIDEOTAPE.

Police Officer Megan Cox tells her story: We were up on

the second floor and we were, we were clearing the building after one night of that haunted house had been open. And we were clearing from the top down. We got to the second floor, it was my first time in the building, all the guards said stand against the walls, which we did. And at that time there was a light that just went across the whole room and it scared everybody to death.

During my interviews, there was none more enjoyable then with Joe. Mr. Joe Mattingly being Charlie's Dad was in his eighties. We asked him to tell us of some of his experiences when he worked there as a orderly in the late thirties.

What was actually your job?
What would did you do?
You would feed people right?
Joe: I tried it all....
You did it all? and you worked at
Waverly in nineteen thirty....six?
Joe: Thirty seven....

Thirty seven you worked here for three years? Oh....what a trip.
Was it scary back then? Did the place seem scary at all?

Joe dare not answer.....

PARANORMAL INVESTIGATION 168-WHS SECOND FLOOR INVESTIGATION DATA
REASON FOR SUSPECT: ODORS   POSSIBLE TARGETS: 2   AVERAGE EMF
READINGS: 10 TO 18 M-GAUSS   EVP-CHECK DATA   IRT READINGS-
TEMPERATURE: 78   HUMIDITY: 13   COLD SPOTS DETECTED: 1   HOT SPOTS
DETECTED: UNKNOWN   PARANORMAL PHENOMENA: ORBS
VISUAL PHENOMENA: UNKNOWN

SECOND FLOOR IDENTIFIED HUMAN ODORS. COLD SPOTS DETECTED. TEMPERATURES 40 AND 50 DEGREES AND DROPPING

But it was after our initial inspection that we heard several footsteps around us, the sound of a door closing and the smell of fresh baked bread in the air. There was no logical explanation for these things. They simply happened and several of us were there to witness them.

Early in the mornings you'll smell food cooking. I mean it's like bacon and eggs and blueberry muffins and in the afternoon fried chicken and you are just wondering where is that coming from. Because there is nothing around here. You shouldn't smell those smells.

Ron Parkhurst use to do security for Waverly Hills a few years back. He recalls his experience on the second floor: You know oddly enough, last year, I remember that one day, I actually smelt food. And I am not going to say one thing or another, but I remember I was standing in this second floor hallway probably half way down, almost to the point of being in the west wing and I could literally identify certain smells. Gravy Bacon Eggs.

Logan: About Six or seven o'clock in the morning, we can smell breakfast cooking in the kitchen.

Alecia: Yeah, actually smell them cooking breakfast lunch, dinner. *"Do you smell that? Someone's making breakfast."*

Logan: Most of the time it's pancakes or something like that. Something bakery and I mean, it's a distinct smell to where you can smell just like that,... and there's nothing.

Look at those ovens. Wow. Along here somewhere was a regular kitchen stove and at a certain time the baking was done here and they'd keep those doors open to keep the patients warm.

Each wing of Waverly on each floor has a small dining area, where somebody, if they could get out of bed but couldn't be out of bed very long, they could go to the little dining room in their wing and eat a meal there. Later when they got to a higher level of recovery and needed exercise they would go to the main cafeteria and eat in that dining room which was separated by folding doors and had two separate dining rooms. One huge one and a smaller one where from the pictures I've seen seems to be where the children for the most part ate.

The main dining room capacity could seat 328 employees and, or patients at one sitting. The room could be expanded to seat 448 people at once. An average of 2,100 meals were served daily.

They weren't allowed to go out into the public, and the reason being is because they could contaminate and spread the disease more than what it was.

Ex-patient Delores Webster shares her tender story:
Some people.... Not my family, but some people's sat across the room about 40 feet away, afraid of you. Like, I had an episode, and it hurt my feelings but then I understand now, someone asked are you going to be friends with Delores after she gets out of here, He said, I certainly will...He said I love her. He said, not her fault she was sick. So, some people really didn't understand.

Joe Mattingly: And the people that worked in the building, would have to go hang out the window to breathe.

Delores Webster: It's like I told you, sometimes we felt like second class citizens. And we really didn't tell people about our illness. We came up here to Waverly Hills. I wasn't ashamed of it, but I just didn't tell them.

Either I go where there is peace or I get better, hope is all we have. Hope for a cure.

Where was your favorite place in the whole hospital or sanatorium? Where was your favorite place that you used to like to go?..... or you didn't like to go?

Joe Mattingly: It wasn't... It wasn't for me.... I wasn't the type of person who liked any part of this that's the reason I quit.

An interesting fact; Author George Orwell was dying from tuberculosis as he struggled to complete the frightening tale, "1984" From the novel's gloomy theme, one can recognize his life in a sanatorium. Orwell's illness is present in his book, in the oppressiveness of the atmosphere. You can sense the sadness of what was happening to him! A dark read indeed.

Was it depressing? Sad?

Joe Mattingly: Yeah... I was busy most of the time, see when you work here, you see everything. It's a little bit different as I didn't have an executive job, I had a labor job,you know.

Sometimes you see more that way though.

Yeah you sure do

But you don't say anything....

Cathy Gales ex-Woodhaven nurse remembers the horror: You could hear noises up on other floors, and there were times when you could hear screams and moans and you know they weren't coming from your patients, but I tried to get up on one of the floors one time and I almost got fired.

Joe Mattingly: Worst job I ever had in my life, they had a

big tray, a big rack, and they had trays on there, and you had to take that and roll that truck up here and take off the tray and take two of them in, if they was asleep you'd wake them up turn them over, set the tray in front of them... one day of that and I said, I'm quitting.... I won't do that job. That's the worst job in the world....

The way Author George Orwell described "Big Brother" was exactly the way rules used to be applied in a TB sanatorium.

The Rules of a Sanatorium

7:15 -Rising Bell 8:00 to 8:30 -Breakfast 8:30 to 11:00 -Rest or Exercise as Ordered 11:00 to 12:45 -Rest on Bed 1:00 to 1:30 -Dinner 1:45 to 4:00 -Rest on Bed, Reading but no talking allowed. Quiet Hour 4:00 to 5:45 -Rest or Exercise as Ordered 6:00 -Supper 8:00 -Nourishment if Ordered 9:00 -All Patients in pavilions 9:30 -All Lights Out

Education of the people and through them of the state is the first and greatest need in the prevention of Tuberculosis.

Theres a lot of ghost stories about this place, a lot of rumors of it being haunted, but more importantly it's like the place is haunting. Like for some reason the history is just wanting to be told.

THE THIRD FLOOR

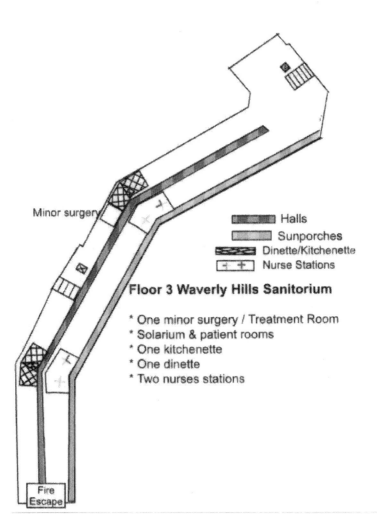

Unidentified bldg
on roof of 2nd Floor

Minor surgery

Halls
Sunporches
Dinette/Kitchenette
Nurse Stations

Floor 3 Waverly Hills Sanitorium

* One minor surgery / Treatment Room
* Solarium & patient rooms
* One kitchenette
* One dinette
* Two nurses stations

Fire
Escape

52

Philip Booth director of Sony Picture's *Death Tunnel*
recalls what it was like to film inside Waverly Hills:

I was walking back, we were filming the sequence where a
little girl flashbacks into the 1930's, and I was walking to the set,
down the long hallway I saw this blur like if I was gonna do it
justice and describe it, it would be holographic, a little girl in a
dress, went right through a wall.

I didn't know what to say, I saw it, I knew I saw it, one of
the security guards came up to me and looked at me and said, *"You
saw her didn't you?"* And I went, *"How do you know?"* and she
goes, *"You saw Mary"*, I said *"Yeah!"* She said *"Well I knew that
cause we heard her giggling this morning."* They said that
nonchalant, like it happens everyday, and then, it took me about 45
minutes to get composure. To realize, OK...accept this you know
you've seen one now, that's it, continue shooting the movie.

Another spooky part to this story is the prop master, James.
He explains why she ran into that particular wall.

*"She ran in there, well you know why she ran in there don't
you"*, I said *"No...why?"* He says, *"Come look."* And on the table,
was this broken statue of an identical little girl holding a doll.

*There is a little girl on the Third floor, she's really
creepy, she has no eyes as I have seen it....*

-Christopher Saint Booth

There has also been many reports of people peeking out of the third story window where most of the patients lived. Most often, what resembles the likeness of a Little Girl!

Keith Age, Louisville Ghost Hunter tells us his experience: Well one day a psychic found her way through the guards before they got good security up here. Made her way up to this bathroom right over here. Got into a crawl space and came out with three old time pictures, the three pictures was of three boys sitting on a rock somewhere another one took a picture while they were moving in a car, and the third picture was a school picture of a little girl, about the way a lot of people describe Mary as they see her running through the third floor here in the solarium, and on the bottom in pencil is written Love Mary Lee. Now, whether Mary Lee really exists or not, we don't know. We've got photos of things that might be a little girl, might be a little boy, we don't know. So until we can finally get some absolute proof, this is where hopefully Mary stays until we can get some more proof.

These is also a ball that everyone keeps talking about. It is known that a little girl has been seen bouncing her ball on the third floor through the hallway. A girl, a girl that was not normal, people kept saying that she had no eyes. It really freaked some of the locals out as they said they would never come back up to this building again.

HE ENCOUNTERED WHAT HE SAID WAS A GIRL, A GIRL THAT WAS NOT NORMAL, HE KEPT SAYING SHE HAD NO EYES.

"Never again, never", stated a local musician who routinely broke into Waverly Hills Sanatorium. "Only once, in my life have I ever heard a little girl laugh and with a ball and that was in Waverly and that was enough for me."

Why won't anybody play with me? I just wanna play!

We have many pictures of the hallway and it looks like there could be a ball in these pictures or a possible light abnormality.

Tina Mattingly owner of Waverly Hills Sanatorium speaks out: I have seen a ball in the building, I have had it roll to me. I don't know where it came from, It just suddenly came rolling down the hallway when no one else was in the building. I don't bother it. I would just, you know, leave it alone.

Keith Age adds: The first year I did a tour here, picture the floor with about a foot and a half full of garbage, dust and dirt, twenty years worth. I had a bad habit of walking backwards and talking. On the third floor, where we left the glow stick down there, I tripped over something and landed on my butt, and when I got up to see what it was, and when I got up to see what it was, it was a little leather ball.

So we took that ball, it was the last tour of the night, we took it and brought it up here to the fourth floor. Took it over here to the operating room. We dropped it off, finished the tour, got done and came back up. The ball was gone. We found it down on the second floor.

PARANORMAL INVESTIGATION   168-WHS THIRD FLOOR INVESTIGATION DATA   REASON FOR SUSPECT: HAUNTING   MISSING GIRL   POSSIBLE TARGETS: 6   AVERAGE EMF READINGS: 56 TO 90 M-GUASS   EVP- YOUNG GIRL, BALL   SOUND   IRT READINGS TEMPERATURE: 57   HUMIDITY: 18   COLD SPOTS   DETECTED: 2 HOT SPOTS DETECTED: 2   PARANORMAL PHENOMENA: SPIRIT   VISUAL PHENOMENA: HIGH LEVEL   APPARITION- PRESENT

THIRD FLOOR. SUSPECTED HAUNTING. EVP. ORBS AND SHADOW PEOPLE. HAUNT ACTIVE

The third floor is where the little girl is supposedly been seen several times. There is a little girl who will come and ask you to play with her.

If you fear ghosts or not, once your up here for a while you don't really fear the ghosts, you just accept them!

A Waverly Hills eye witness speaks out: "She looked probably about six or seven, it was like she was wrapped around the window sill trying to figure out what was going on."

Tina Mattingly continues: A volunteer and I were walking down about two o'clock in the morning and we heard what sounded like a small child, a little girl, say hello. And he looked at me and I looked at him and he said, did you hear that? I said, What did you hear. He said I heard a little girl say hello. I said that is what I heard, and we both was like, let's get out of here.

And then I had one patient, Cathy Gales adds, that she would always be talking to somebody. And I'd ask her who she was talking to. She told me she was talking to this little girl. She'd tell me that this little girl told her that she was gonna be coming and taking her. And I just figured, well, with her being an older person that, you know, she was just seeing things. Three days after she told me that this little girl came, she died.

November 30, 1998 - We were taking pictures of the outside when my friend saw what we originally came to find. In the third floor at the 5th window on the right side of the building we all saw a young female child just staring at us.

-Nurse Cathy Gales

THE FOURTH FLOOR

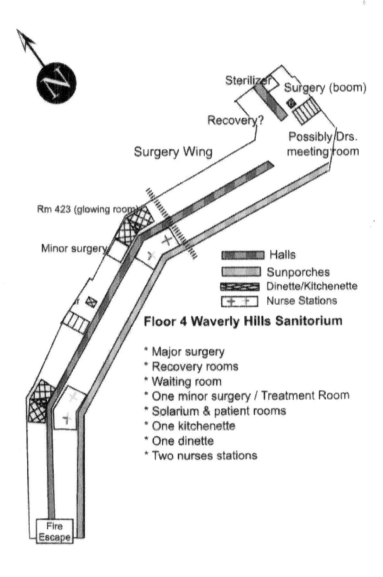

Sterilizer   Surgery (boom)

Recovery?

Surgery Wing   Possibly Drs. meeting room

Rm 423 (glowing room)

Minor surgery

▬▬▬ Halls
▭▭▭ Sunporches
▨▨▨ Dinette/Kitchenette
[+ +] Nurse Stations

Floor 4 Waverly Hills Sanitorium

* Major surgery
* Recovery rooms
* Waiting room
* One minor surgery / Treatment Room
* Solarium & patient rooms
* One kitchenette
* One dinette
* Two nurses stations

Fire Escape

W hat was on the third floor? I don't know I was always on the fourth floor. - Patient Delores Webster.

The fourth floor, is where they did their operations and kept all their sickest patients close to death.

Waverly owner Charles Mattingly gives us some facts: The upper class people with the money who could afford the exploratory surgeries, they went to the fourth floor. And they were given the... whatever you want to call it... given the royal treatment.

Douglas Steele: Waverly Hills used to, back then, do a lot of research.

Charles Mattingly: This hospital always had a waiting list to get in. It never had any empty beds in it at all. And from what we understand people came in as far as 500 miles away to come to this facility because it was known for its cutting edge technology and their exploratory surgery.

Patient Delores Webster sighs: What I had was called Pneumothorax. New ways of resting the lung have been developed. This patient is getting Pneumothorax treatment. Air is let into the chest cavity and that rests the lung so that it can heal. When the diseased lung is fully healed, it is allowed to expand again.

New ways of resting the lung have been developed. This patient is getting Pneumothorax treatment. Air is let into the chest cavity and that rests the lung so that it can heal.

When the diseased lung is fully healed, it is allowed to expand again.....

- Public message

Delores Webster: And they were cutting and they said, held my hands and now you can scream and you can yell but don't you dare move cause it was right by my heart. And I remember it was so hot in there, They didn't have air conditioning.

Charles Mattingly: What the operation consisted of was they would come in and they would cut open your rib cage, actually remove a few of your ribs, they would take and collapse the lung that was in the worst shape and they would keep you calm as possible and have you breathe off of your good lung hoping that your other lung, while they had it collapsed would start to regenerate and get in better shape. Then they'd come back later and puff it back up and see if it took. A lifesaver for many.

Patient Douglas Steele: In this instance, you go in and reset a portion of the ribcage, and that allows the whole chest wall to cave in.

Charles Webster was a patient at Waverly Hills and had the horrific operation or experiment?: My right side... They took parts of five ribs... about that much out of each rib....five of them. To collapse the lung......It makes you walk sideways because you're out of balance, you know.....You're always...trying to favor that side, but I don't of course anymore, but when I first had it done I was walking down the street sideways. Trying to get away from it I guess....the pain...That's a pretty good pain.

From the December 1940 issue of the Waverly Bulletin, a in house newspaper that was written for the staff and patients by the staff and patients at Waverly Hills.

CHEST PAIN

By: Lawrence A. Taugher, M.D.

When the doctor makes his daily rounds, the two most frequently encountered complaints are: "Doctor, I have a headache" and I have a pain in my chest". Now, let's take a little aspirin for the headaches and forget them and then let's see what causes the chest pains.

First of all, practically all of these chest pains are not severe enough to require medication. The main element is fear, fear that the pain indicates some activity of tuberculosis and when assured that such is not the case more patients feel better immediately and can laugh the whole thing off.

Now we want to know how to tell which pains are worth

bothering about and which are not. Well, the only tuberculous activity which actually causes definite pain is pleurisy. This pleuritic pain is sharp and stabbing and comes with almost every breath and is much worse if you take an unusually deep breath. Remember that this pleurisy is due to infection of the pleura causing inflammation and this in turn causes a rise in temperature. Here is a pint worth remembering. If the pain is not accompanied by a rise in temperature, and I mean more than 99 or 99.2, roll over an go to sleep; it just isn't anything to worry about.

For the few people who will find cause for worry in the fore-going lets see if there isn't a silver lining some place. First of all, if you have to have Tb. Then you had better have it in the pleura than in your lung because it is much less serious and usually quiets down much more quickly. Some doctors even claim that the pleural fluid increases the resistance of the lung itself. Pleural effusions which appear following a pneumothorax or the cutting of adhesions are often times not seen due to infection but rather to the irritating effect of the air or the burning thru of the adhesions. This fluid is a terrible nuisance yet in nine cases out of ten that is all it is – just a nuisance.

So far we've covered only the pains due to inflammation and let's repeat again, these are comparatively few and far between. The common variety are best described as indefinite, small, sharp pains and aches which are more or less persistent while they last and are not affected by breathing. These are the kind which neither you or I can put our finger on exactly. Some of these are caused by a momentary plugging of a small bronchial tube by a piece of mucous or pus which causes a sharp cramping sensation but is relieved as soon as the plug passes along. The vast majority of the other aches and pains could be truthfully called "healing pains" in as much as they are due to nature's own effort toward healing disease and result from the contraction of scar tissue in your lung an pleura. As the disease heals a scar forms and as the scar grows older it shrinks and pulls on the structures adjacent to it. The same thing occurs when the diaphragm has just been paralyzed and again later when it begins to move; at first the lung and abdominal organs are pulled one way and later they are pulled back. It is this pulling which causes the pain and while we wish that you didn't have to have them yet, you and I ought both agree that if most chest pains are good signs instead of bad ones, then "Here's to Pain."

They called this monster the White Death, the White Plague for the simple fact that you couldn't create enough red blood cells from your oxygen.

I only weighed 79 pounds...and I was pretty sick.

-Delores Webster

Because that is what TB does, it attacks your red blood cells in your lungs. So what they did was, people that was going to be dying, they did not want to leave these ghastly white corpses, they didn't want their family to remember them by that so they would take them into these, this room right here and these are the first tanning salons in America.

Douglas Steele: They had one big room up there, they called a lamp room. This was a room that only had ultraviolet of this type of lamp.

Charles Mattingly: They would bring the patients in here before they would get the visitors to come in and they would put them under the sun lamp that they were forced to try to get some color back into their skin.

Now they did use heat lamps on patients. I have seen pictures of them. Where they would have their clothing pushed back, and would have a heat lamp on their back. you know, on their lungs. Cause they did think the heat would help.

They also thought that fresh air, even cold air was better for you than stagnant air, that is why they called this the open air hospital.

In the winter time they would even have snow at the foot of their beds. The patients would be out here even in the middle of winter when there was snow on the ground. Snow was coming through the screens as the patients would be bundled up trying to them some fresh air.

Douglas Steele: I spent the winter of 1939 out on the porch where there were four other people and me. Five of us out on an open porch in the wintertime. The only thing we had between us and the weather was a tarpaulin, that could be drawn and pulled across on a metal cable.

Charles Webster: Of course out on that porch it was cold. Only blankets....   *Brrrrrr!*

Basically they didn't know what to do. They were just trying to help people and doing whatever they thought would help.

Delores Webster: They used to put sandbags on their chests while they were lying to take bed rest.... I don't know what that would do?.......

Douglas Steele: A lot of things they did then they thought was effective was just doing the wrong thing.

There is always hope inside ones soul. The heart can not give up but sometimes the body does. Below are some letters from a patient to her loved one while being admitted to Waverly Hills Sanatorium. With the utmost and deepest respect I present them below, as I day in the life of the infected.....

LETTER 1

November 12, 1945

Dearest Annie,

I don't feel equal to more than a few lines so will make it sorta brief. I haven't written you since I was fluoroscoped last, have I ? As you know, my cough, expectoration, temp and what have you, have been the limit. Doctor was giving me APC tablets and also changed my cough medicine, so I don't know which it is or whether its either but I have 4, 5 or 6 spells of cramping a day, cramps like you had diarrhea, except I haven't yet. Now I'm wondering if its intestinal TB, ovarian trouble, kidney trouble or what, plus a sore throat that I've suffered a week with. Not the usual sore throat, but a hoarseness, throbbing, aching throat. It too could be TB. I'm up for an exam by the surgeon. I dread it. No breakfast, dope you, numb your throat, then probe around.....Since he (The Doctor) took me off APC my temp has gone back to 101+. But heres the last report, one of the lesions has shelled out into a cavity, but he insists, saying "Be positive, I'm healing, looking better." That sounds crazy, but can be explained this way, I am healing around the outer edge (where you begin to heal) but the center has shelled out. I'm not not too discouraged for this reason, sometimes after an old lesion shells out the cavity heals quicker than the lesion. However, if it doesn't, I'm still in the same boat 'cause the operation will take care of the trouble as it is now as well as before. So, I don't mind the lying here if I didn't feel so awful, all I can do is wait and bear it as patiently as possible. I have never had a very good feeling about getting well this time, but we won't discuss that. So much for that. ....

I must close cause my head is splitting open. Its visiting day and visitors and other people don't improve my curing. I'm almost afraid to lie on my left side because of drainage into that side from the right.........

Love and take care of yourself,

Ella Reed

LETTER 2

November 15, 1946

Dear Ann,

Since one little sheet of paper is all I have (except 3 or 4 for emergency) I guess I'll have to write small and be brief. ...... how it will all turn out I don't know. Anyway my one prayer is that mother has not developed TB. I think I could bear almost anything else, but to have accusing fingers pointing at me would be more than my sick mind could stand........ The weather here is still nice, but each day I expect the worse. I know its nice there and I wish I could be there, those memories are very pleasant and I wish I could be privileged to enjoy more......... Now shall I talk about me or would that be better left unsaid? As you may or may not know according to family reports, I am not better. My cough is just about as bad as anyone's could be, however I have it seemingly under control where it doesn't bother me too much. Then my temp, except for a period, enduring the beginnings of my kidney infection, my temp is usually normal in the morning AM but in the PM afternoon and evening it ranges from 99.6 to 101. Most of the time hovering around 100 which I'm very proud of. But I have this pain in the kidney or bladder which had not cleared up and after a week of medicine and three tests. I don't know how high the infection is but enough I suppose. Dr. C. said they examined for TB and it was not TB but the result of toxic poisoning, high temp. etc. My feet are swollen to my (including) ankles... some minutes or hours puffed like a balloon then next only slight swelling around the ankles. ......I am losing protein through the kidneys. ......In spite of it all id feel fair, if it wasn't for the nausea. It strikes anytime of the day and I usually lie here and cry, then a few moments of serene comfort. It's just that I know that the cause of my kidney condition (which is TB) can not be corrected at this time. Consequently you see my chances. I believe that earthly physicians are powerless to do one thing more at this particular time and that only God's healing power can take care of it. ...... Mother, I sure do miss her. I was in hopes of getting my hair washed with this liquid stuff they washed Grandma's in. I asked mother but she conveniently forgot it. Of course I understand, yet I've never accepted that fact that shes afraid to touch me. I don't suppose she's touched me once or twice in all these weeks. She very willingly hands me a bed pan and a glass of water (with the two fingers she uses). I've also asked Rachel to please roll a dozen or so pin curls (it hasn't been rolled since August) but do you think she will? She's either too tired , not enough time or something, oh well, I can't write any more. ......

Love, Ellie Reed

LETTER 3

Dear Sis,

I don't feel equal to writing more than a few lines so here goes. Do enjoy every single note I get from you, so keep me well informed. Received your note today. Glad everything is okay. I don't know what mother and family write you about my condition but don't be fooled by any of them. I'm a "mighty sick chick" and if there isn't a change soon I'm willing to bet my time is measured in weeks... months at the most. Im sure she's (mother) written you about my cross disposition. It is bad but please remember there are two sides to every question. I neither have the strength nor heart to say all the things I'd like you to know. Above everything else, give me credit for realizing the sacrifices she and the rest of the family have made. But don't forget, I've paid dearly for them. I couldn't have stood it without someone near but its meant setting me back a year. Don't let any of this worry you because one of two things are bound to happen. Either I go where there is peace or else I get better and more able to bear my cross. ...... Didn't tell you, my body is so swollen I can hardly turn it over. Waist just 36 inches, hips about 40 or more. Feet look like clubs...enough of this.

Goodnight and sweet dreams,

With all my love,
Ellie Reed

In memory of Ella Reed Norris 1906-1947
Daughter of Reed and Daisy Sharp Norris
Sister of Anna Norris.
Resident of Louisville, Kentucky.

PARANORMAL INVESTIGATION   167-WHS FORTH FLOOR INVESTIGATION DATA
REASON FOR SUSPECT: DEATHS   UNSOLVED MURDERS   POSSIBLE TARGETS: 5
AVERAGE EMF READINGS: 26 TO 46 M-GAUSS   EVP-CHECK DATA
IRT READINGS-TEMPERATURE: 52   HUMIDITY: 13   COLD SPOTS DETECTED: 3
HOT SPOTS DETECTED: UNKNOWN   PARANORMAL PHENOMENA: ORBS
VISUAL PHENOMENA: UNKNOWN

FOURTH FLOOR. DANGEROUSLY ACTIVE. BARBARIC OPERATIONS. NO HUMAN LIFE. HAUNT ACTIVE.

Keith Age: This is the most active place we got, its here on the fourth floor. This is the room temp. It is laser guided. As you can see... 72....and a while ago we were getting readings down in the sixties. And that's what these gadgets are used for...if you find a cold spot, you try to document it with this.

So what we got is...we got an air pressure change, we got cool air coming up on us, and the way breezes and things work, if there was going to be a breeze in here it would be going down. This thing is like the wind just sucks it out plus the temperature has just dropped ten degrees. But it's only on one side. Over here it's 63 degrees.

See now right down here....62 degrees.....73... ten degree difference......It's bouncing back and forth...I'll try here now. It's moving, the cold spot's moving.

Charles Mattingly: In the middle of the night we see rooms

start to glow. That we can't explain. We see shadows move around, and these are all things we can't find a reason for them happening.

Keith Age: Hey guys, want to see something really cool? Look here! These doors have been locked up and look what we got! What have we got?

Footprints....see it? Not only that, it's a bare foot print.

December 30, 2000-The huge steel door that i had just kicked to get open, opened and slammed shut three times, once we got into the hallway. All three of us watched as this huge door swing open then shut by itself! I have not since been into the hospital and honestly have no plans of returning.
-Waverly Hills Visitor.

You've got to have some serious courage to break in here and monkey around and really investigate and thoroughly look for evidence of any kind of afterlife activities. Especially in a place like this that is so notorious for operations and the illness and the plague.

We all went up one night on the fourth floor which is supposed to be the most haunted. And we all turned off our flashlights and it was late at night. And we just stood there. And we saw like this weird thing of light.

I went up to the fourth floor one night, at night, I am not sure what time it was, you know in the wee hours of the night. I went up with a group of people and it was my first time up there and I was seeing shadows and strange lights.

-Annie Burgstede-Actress

Kinda bouncing around, and we all saw the same thing. There was no reflection or anything it was just like this weird ball of light.

Joe: You know, anybody ever tell you they had a crazy house on the other end up at the top?

THE FIFTH FLOOR

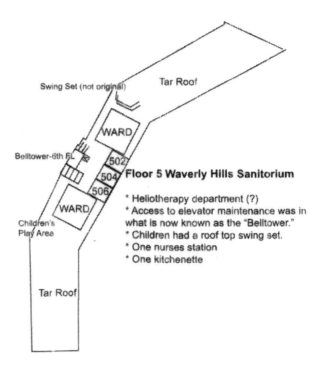

Floor 5 Waverly Hills Sanitorium

* Heliotherapy department (?)
* Access to elevator maintenance was in what is now known as the "Belltower."
* Children had a roof top swing set.
* One nurses station
* One kitchenette

74

The 5th floor was also a children's ward and insane ward for hard to manage Patients. Hopefully not at the same time.

Charles Matttingly: On the fifth floor, that was known as the sunrooms up there. And my dad described the roof up there...

Joe Mattingly: That was for people that was all... You had to have somebody with you go up there, they would knock you in the head some of them. They'd come up and grab you.

Mr. Thornbury: Now, the fifth floor wasn't very big.

Charles Mattingly: It was divided into two parts. Some of the patients that had maybe some mental problems,or bothered some of the other patients during the day they would take their bed and roll it to the elevator and take them up to the fifth floor and stick them out to one side of the sunroom to keep them away from the general population if they were bothering them too much.

Charles Webster: Yeah, it was just like you were outside. I really liked it because I was nature bound anyhow. They put us on the fifth floor, where you had just a little more freedom there. Just a great big solarium.

This is the wing on the fifth floor where the mentally insane TB patients lived at and where they stored them at. We ask our Spooked cast, locals and employees of Waverly Hills....

"What do you know about the fifth floor? Who knows the stories about the fifth floor?"

Dan, a local hard rock musician: Well, in the first shower stall, there was these scratch marks, in the tile. You know, and I'm thinking now how the hell did this happen?

Mr. Thornbury: I know but I'd rather not say.

Room 502 has gotten a lot of publicity, you have Incursion 502, the local band, which, according to rumors they got the 502 in their name from that room. It doesn't make a lot of sense to me, like I have discussed before, an incursion is a hostile takeover, why would anyone want to do a hostile takeover in a bathroom of an abandoned hospital?

Tina Mattingly: Well, it's local teenagers, made Room 502 a big thing.

Cathy Gales: There was rumors going around that a nurse had hung herself up there.

Dan: The whole reason behind it is I took the numbers off the door, Room 502 and whatever spirit lurks in there didn't appreciate it very much. Every place I took the numbers.. I brought them home, I got kicked out of my house. I brought them to our practice spot and we got kicked out of there. So finally I gave them to our guitar player and now they are on the front of his guitar cabinet.

PARANORMAL INVESTIGATION 167-WHS FIFTH FLOOR INVESTIGATION DATA
REASON FOR SUSPECT: PHANTOMS   TWO SUICIDE RELATED DEATHS   POSSIBLE
TARGETS: 4   AVERAGE EMF READINGS: 50 TO 80 M-GAUSS   EVP- FAINT
FEMALE CRYING   IRT READINGS-TEMPERATURE: 45   HUMIDITY: 15   COLD
SPOTS DETECTED: NUMEROUS   HOT SPOTS DETECTED: 4   PARANORMAL
PHENOMENA: ORBS   VISUAL PHENOMENA: HIGH LEVEL ECTO-VAPOR- PRESENT

FIFTH FLOOR. ECTOPLASM AND VAPOR VISIBLE.
SUGGESTED SUICIDAL TENDENCIES.

Steffany Huckaby/Death Tunnel actress: You know when we went up to the fifth floor, we were only up there for like 15 minutes. And it affected me for two full days.

Back in the 40's, this is during the TB days, a nurse, so depressed over the conditions of people dying up here from tuberculosis, took her own life by hanging herself.

Local Girl: Yeah, I heard she hung herself while she was pregnant.

Douglas Steele: No, I never heard that.

It is said that every woman that walks into that room... feels if........... they're pregnant.

Philip Booth/Filmmaker: And the EMF meter goes crazy right?

Local Girl: Yeah. They get completely sick like they have to walk out of the room.

Keith Age: This room reacts to women who have been up here who were pregnant. The first time we ever came up here, Tina Mattingly was also with us, we pulled out an EMF meter and it was mid july, it was hot, muggy, but all of the sudden it went from 86 degrees to 98 degrees in three seconds. The EMF meter went off, it just went crazy, it melted the solder right out of the back of it.

Tina Mattingly: And I do know for a fact there was a nurse that supposedly committed suicide on the fifth floor.

Douglas Steele: Now I can't say that it didn't happen. Now we had a patient that was there that slashed her wrists.

Keith Age: Now what we do know for a fact in 1926 the first head nurse hung herself. We got the death record and it was ruled a suicide. What we do know is that she was basically 27 years old, unmarried and pregnant. So that is why she probably did hang herself. She hung herself from... there used to be a different light fixture in here, she sat here and hung, there were 12 hour shifts at that time, so basically she hung for 12 hours while the patients here on this side sat here and watched her.

The infamous Room 502, was where unfortunately a nurse discovered she was pregnant out of wedlock.

Mr. Thornbury: She made a mistake.... Got Pregnant.... Killed herself.

It was said that she performed self surgery on herself and unfortunately aborted the illegitimate child and then...

Mr. Thornbury: They showed us, where they found that baby.

We did find information from the coroner that I believe it was in 1932 a stillborn baby was found on Pages Lane said Waverly historian John Amerine

Ron Parkhurst: That was the first rumor that I heard. The second version was that she possibly jumped out a window.

THE WHITE DOG

People have asked me repeatedly whether I had heard or witnessed the story of the homeless man and his white dog. Well I can honestly say, a big YES! Several versions of this story were told to me by the metro police department who monitored the security, patrolling the area late at night. This story was also backed up by the locals and the Waverly Hills caretakers.

The story starts as a lonely old vagrant supposedly a

veteran made a temporary home in the deteriorated Waverly Hills Sanatorium. Sporting long red hair and a beard, he was poorly thin yet tall. His tattered old army coat earned his ghostly name as "The Veteran". Accompanied by his trusted companion a large White Dog, he was known to stay on the fifth floor next to the elevator shaft. One night this old chap was awoken by a girl screaming from below possibly the first floor of Waverly. Upon his investigation he witnessed three teenage boys raping a young girl.

It was known that after Woodhaven shut down that Satanic cults would break in regularly the sanatorium to practice their dark magic and rituals. These boys may have been apart of a gang or a coven, either way they beat him to death. They also killed his white dog as they bludgeoned the animal as if in a rhythmic ritual.

Both the man and dog had satanic symbols carved in their bodies. Both the dog and homeless man was then carried up to the fifth floor and pushed down the elevator shaft. As there are no public records of this incident, the boys were eventually caught but were underage so their identities were concealed and the story hidden, remaining a legend.

Many people see 'The Veteran" roaming the halls of Waverly while others hear barking, panting and scratching sounds of his white phantom dog.

There has been alternate reports that said the homeless man

had raped this young girl while she was exploring the abandoned building. Shortly after that she told her three brothers of what happened and they came back. Late one night the family hunted him down and threw him and his dog down the elevator shaft.

Either way the White Dog story indeed exists.

THE BONE DUMP

A memory that will never fade as it is as creepy as it is awakening. Back in 2003 we were filming our Sony Pictures horror film, Death Tunnel on location at Waverly Hills Sanatorium. One night after our regular 18 hour shooting days, I returned back to our hotel. We stayed at many different hotels when we were there, just outside of downtown Louisville, by the airport. Arriving back at the hotel lobby I quickly went to the hotel desk to ask for my key. One of the hardest things to keep track of, beside sunglasses, are hotel keys as I always seem to misplace them somewhere in limbo where all my lost socks are. When approaching the hotel desk the night manager spoke. " Hey you all are the ones doing Death Tunnel?...., have you bin to the Bone Dump yet?" Alarmed that all the locals seemed well aware that we were filming at Waverly due to the recent front page and center spread in the Courier Times entertainment section, I not so-immediately answered. Being very tired from our long day of shooting. I eventually answered. "What, what are you talking about?" Out of shock that I did not know where this golden coral smorgasbord of bodies were, he proceeded to fill me in with the menu.

Apparently there is a place when Waverly Hills Sanatorium changed over to Woodhaven (the old folks home) that they disposed of all of there stuff such as bottles, needles, bedpans etc. Realizing that TB was a contagious and infective disease, this seemed to be a BIG problem for the local EPA, the Environmental Protection Agency then something we could go and film.

It was rumored that a lot of bones from bodies were buried there as well giving birth to the legend and the name the.....

"BONE DUMP!"

Being a documentarian with a strong back bone in the search for the truth and a good story, we decided to check this story and place out. The local night manager proceeded in his Kentucky drawl to tell us where to find this gruesome place ending by drawing a kindergarden map of the Bone Dump location on a hotel napkin.

Well you could imagine at that point this hotel desk odd conversation made it a possible to 'NOT' have a good nights sleep.

The very next morning was the perfect time to head out and

find this infamous bone yard. Following the makeshift recycled napkin map we arrived on the outside of Waverly Hills Sanatorium. Wrecking alone except for a dear friend into the woods we passed the Golf Course that was once rumored to be built over a large unmarked cemetery. We must of walked at least two miles in as each step got deeper into the creep zone. A forest began a slight take over as at this point I started to feel one could get lost.

We passed several strange trees. Trees that were bearing a strange fruit, that fruit being 'raw fear.' The trees were deformed at their base as the trunks circled out to almost resembling the letter L backwards. There is much folk lore about how trees like this even exist. Whether by witches, devils or man made by Native Americans used a trail markers. They are an incredible sight.

Trail Marker Trees are trees that were intentionally shaped by Native Americans throughout North America with distinctive characteristics that convey that the tree was shaped by man rather than a tree simply deformed by nature or disease.

http://stevecreek.com/native-american-trail-marker-tree

Completely spooked by now, we came across some broken china plates in the woods. The plates were a faded white with blue logos on them. The logo was a straight initial design with a blue stamp with the letters WHS, Waverly Hills Sanatorium.

BOOM....We found it. Here was a path of broken plates leading to the infamous Bone Dump! As we embarked to the top of the hill there she was, a rustic mound of IV bottles, bedpans, shoes, medicine bottles and lots of bones. The locals assured me that they were animal bones not human bones as they would have to report them if they were human. Personally I found the bones very human looking, some were larger then the others which may have belonged to pigs or other wild stock. Waverly Hills did have their own local live stock though the actual location was unknown.

We found small glass vials and tubes full of dried blood, needles and other medical instruments. The whole thing did not sit well with me as my gut instinct told me that there was more then this place being just a dumping ground. It was obvious it was hazardous but the hospital nor the city did not want to pay for the removal of thus hazardous waste. It was not in anybodies budget though it was in ones best health interest, yet it was never reported.

It was the find of the century, though its discovery in turn fathered a whelm of local trouble after our return. The locals scurried to get rid of the evidence once they knew we found it whether for Waverly Hills souvenirs or to clean up a possible EPA violation causing a temporary close down of the sanatorium's premises. Either way this adventure stains my memory as one of the most dark secrets of Waverly Hills Sanatorium.

THE CREEPER

There is a fascinating story that is floating around about an entity known as The Creeper or aka Shadow Eyes. Well it recently came across my desk. It all started when I received a letter below from a woman (as I can not reveal her name due to her recent passing) that claims to be the last living nurse of Woodhaven Geriatrics Center. Below is that letter.

I am the last living nurse, that was in the ECT treatment room, that day of the Creeper manifestation to protect that child. The Doctors all (blamed the child for the destruction) of the room, but it was not shadow eyes that tore up the room, he was strapped down threw the entire event. And at 89 and now dying, my organs are failing, and now with hospice care. I have to get this off my conscious before I take my last breath, am letting go of a very dark secret I kept in my keep sakes box, a case file and pictures on Shadow Eyes, and his time in the Wood Haven Geriatrics in 1967 to Tina Mattingly at the Waverly Hills Sanatorium. The paranormal Investigators will be beating down her doors for this story and for this I am sorry. Everyone thought "Shadow Eyes' the child Clair-sentient, had died from his ECT in 1967 and was dead for the past 50 years. But it came to my attention threw Cathy Gales a former Nurse her self ,that he is alive three months ago. I pray this helps him heal. May God forgive me in my part in this.

......Name With held...

Ok then....... I was not sure at first what to think, I intermediately tried to get a hold of this woman as she sounded desperate and I was extremely worried that she was not completely sound of mind. So I wrote her back unfortunately with no reply. I realize now that she has passed from cancer, RIP.

Off I went to find out everything I could about who and what Shadow Eyes was. Through my extensive research and investigation this final story did not disappoint.

As I understand there was an incident or actually several, where in Woodhaven, there were secretive treatments going on in the basement with children. These treatments consisted of a form of ECT, shock therapy. They would use this on unmanageable patients or troubled lads.

A young boy named Richard from Pikesville, Kentucky was apparently a victim in these treatments. If that was not horrific enough the story continues as being such an empathic beautiful boy, the personal and other children committed personal crimes against this soul. Including a documented rape with a trial being held in 1967.

During one of his ECT treatments the story goes that he lashed out by calling upon dark energy to help save him. Windows smashed, furniture moved and mayhem made itself known. There has been may unexplained events and deaths covered up especially back in the segregated days. Which included an African American janitor thrown of Waverly Hills roof and a young girl murdered in 1910 by the old colored hospital.

During this particular investigation of abuse, the hospital files of three boys were told to be removed and hidden by the doctor in charge. The only file that remains is that of the boy called Richard (Shadow Eyes) in which this woman that had contacted me seems to have.

This is an extreme case of an empathic young soul trying to stay alive at a most vulnerable and contagious time.

It has been said that animals and birds came to his rescue during his stay at Woodhaven. Surrounding the skyline, crows hovered above. Deer and other animals appeared from the woods when Shadow Eyes was in need. His hair and eyes would change color as he knew of Waverly's haunted past. Could he have been a fire-starter of strange, wicked things to come.

Waverly Hills Sanatorium served as a Tuberculosis Hospital from October 17th of 1926 up until 1961. After that point it was closed down for approximately 2 years, remodeled and reopened as Woodhaven Geriatrics Center which was basically a nursing home, and it remained that until 1980 when it closed its doors for good. It also was known to have an enormous amount of deaths pass through its doors into the body chute. This was called the Death Tunnel......

Are you nervous now?

Yes...

Why?

Because I'm standing right in front of the death tunnel....

INTRODUCTION 2

The Body Chute, aka Death Tunnel is a 500 foot tunnel with a rail car system and cement steps that connects to the 1st floor of the main Kirkbride building and to the basement of the original hospital. It was steam heated and it was used at one point in time to bring supplies up. It was also used for employees to walk up to get from the bottom of the hill in the winter months when it was extremely cold and snow was deep. It had two rails just like a railroad track in which carts were attached to move heavy objects. At that time, there was a certain point during the Tuberculosis epidemic that there were up to three people an hour dying. In order to keep the patients from being demoralized at their own kind of impending death the hospital staff would cart the bodies out through the first floor to this tunnel, met with a conveyor belt system that went 500 feet down towards the railroad tracks. There the hearses and trains would pick up the bodies and take them home to their family".

Sporting my signature cowboy hat and a faux fur coat, off I flew from Los Angeles to Louisville, Kentucky. Arriving at Waverly Hills Sanatorium for the very first time, I must admit I was extremely blown away. It was like finding a sunken ship in the dessert. I was totally mesmerized yet scared shitless by this monster of a building. I had seen it only in pictures and now this gothic structure beckoned me to enter, if I dare.

There we met the current owners Charlie and Tina Mattingly. As they showed us around the abandoned property, we toured the five decaying floors with excitement. I felt like I was being watched, every hospital room had its own story. Eighty years of peeling paint, twisted walls, iron staircases and a morgue. You couldn't help but respect this deteriorating oasis for when you walked down the long institutional hallways one could imagine what it was like back in the day. Now near extinction we were here to help save this crumbling location through exposure and donations.

Night fell on the old Sanatorium but the day wasn't over as we still had a lot of work to do. Out of the dark came an ominous figure, somewhat intimidating yet walked with a force to be seen. From the shadows to the moonlight, it was no other than the rock & roll Ghost Hunter Keith Age.

Dressed in a leather vest, hat and jacket he seemed to be protective of his turf. Age and his team the LGHS (Louisville Ghost Hunters Society) were the exclusive in-house investigators of Waverly Hills Sanatorium at that time. They had plenty of stories and evidence they soon would share. I told to him and his team that we were here to film a horror movie and any help they could give us in explaining any paranormal disturbances, would be very much appreciated. The bearded hunter looked at his team, smiled and said, *"Welcome to my world."* Keith Age and I would soon become longtime friends and shoot seven more films together.

Keith went on to tell us more about the history of Waverly Hills Sanatorium and the reoccurring paranormal activity they had witnessed. He talked about shadow people, cold spots, EVPs and light abnormalities. His stories were bone chilling and the evidence they captured backed his claim. Intrigued and now awakened we started to document the possibility of the existence of ghosts, during our filming at Waverly.

Introduction from

THE STRANGE CASE OF DEATH TUNNEL

taken from PARANOIA The Strange Case Of Ghosts, Demons and Aliens.
courtesy of Spooked Productions written by Christopher Saint Booth

www.paranoiabook.com

THE DEATH TUNNEL

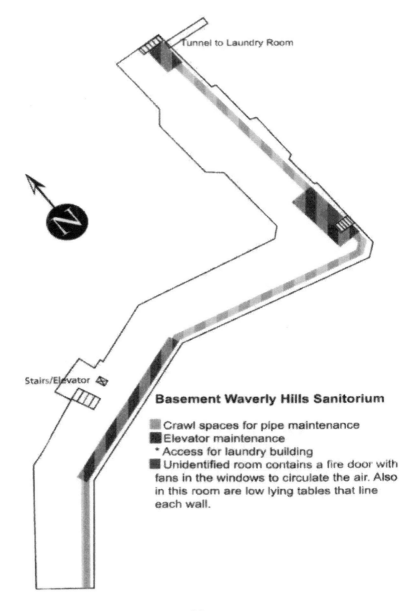

Tunnel to Laundry Room

Stairs/Elevator

Basement Waverly Hills Sanitorium

Crawl spaces for pipe maintenance
Elevator maintenance
* Access for laundry building
Unidentified room contains a fire door with fans in the windows to circulate the air. Also in this room are low lying tables that line each wall.

The Body Chute, aka Death Tunnel is a tunnel with a rail car system and steps that connects to the 1st floor of the main building the basement of the original hospital.

W hen somebody died, they put them in that and then take them down that tunnel.

The death tunnel was is a five hundred foot tunnel dug underground to originally, we feel it was there for supplies to be brought up and keep people warm.

Ron Parkhurst: It was actually a steam tunnel it was steam heated and it was used at one point in time to bring supplies up, it was also used for employees to walk up to get up here from the bottom of the hill in the winter months when it was extremely cold and snow was deep.

Joe Mattingly: It had two rails just like a railroad track, then they got steps. And there's about four or five steps and then there's a flat oh, I'd say maybe 8 feet. And you walk up these steps then you walk on a flat and you walk on another 8 steps and then there's another flat. And that's all the way up that hill.

Ron Parkhurst: But thirdly, it did have a purpose of transporting the bodies of deceased Tb patients.

Philip Booth: There was so many people dying in the hospital that they started putting the bodies down the tunnel so that the other people wouldn't see them.

Sarah Gilbert: At that time there was a certain point during the Tuberculosis epidemic that it was like 3 people an hour were dying and so in order to keep the patients from being demoralized at their own, you know, kind of impending death they would cart the bodies out through the first floor to this death tunnel and it was this conveyor belt system that went 500 feet down towards the railroad tracks and down at the bottom the hearses or the trains would pick up the bodies and take them home to their family.

And you can bet we found that railroad track.

Charles Mattingly: A small like railroad cart, a real small one that would be hoisted up the incline of the hill and bring supplies up and as people died they also used that same cart to lower the bodies down to the bottom of the hill.

Joe Mattingly: And it was like a little railroad cart and they put the bodies on that and let them down there and come back and get another one til they was all gone that they could take. And they'd take them out one at a time.

Mr. Thornbury: The tunnel was built for that reason and to put the morgue down there.

Charles Mattingly: They would lower them all down the hill inside the tunnel so nobody would see them.

Ron Parkhurst: There were people dying frequently in the 30's and 40's.

Charles Mattingly: They would take them out to the railroad cars and load them onto a railroad car or a person could pick them up down there.

Sarah Gilbert: You know they were trying to be very respectful and trying to keep the patients that were alive, you know, kinda try to keep their spirits up and give them some sort of hope for survival. And yet they still had to respectfully had to get the remains of the patients that didn't survive to their homes.

Ron Parkhurst: So they didn't want people to were in this hospital literally seeing people dying every hour. So what they would do is sneak them out through that tunnel down to the bottom and hearses would pick them up.

Mr. Thornbury: There never was but one hearse that ever come up to this building. And the doctor claimed that it upset a patient, and they had this tunnel built right here. and they put that dead wagon right in there.

Hello I'm Roy, I'm a security guard up here at Waverly, and I'll be walking you all through the death tunnel...also known as the locally the body chute.

Cool Let's Go...........

For the first time we will be entering the death tunnel.

Are you scared?

Everybody follow me, Let's go on down the Death Tunnel.

Back when they started with, actually doing tours through caves, people went through caves and started marking the walls. Writing their name and the year they were there in hope to leave a memory of them. You can walk through this tunnel and see pencil marks on the walls. Like for instance there is one right there that states that persons name in 1930........ and another one here 1951.

I mean, there are quite a few of them down through here, but they're getting kind of hard to find. With the water coming in it's eventually eroding them off and wash them off, but there is still a few.   Here is Jane Carol-December 1942...

Charles Mattingly: She told me that she was up here as a nurse and that she was actually here and when she had to leave she had to walk down the tunnel to go down to the little train station there to catch the train to come back into Louisville. And she said as she was going down they was lowering bodies down. She said she actually saw... she actually saw the bodies going down.

Mr. Thornberry: The tunnel was built for that reason and to put the morgue down there.

Douglas Steele: It's not a pleasant thing to think about. I agree, the tunnel. But it is sort of bad, thing to think about. But the tunnel was there for a purpose, and it was no worse than having a morgue.

They would lower them all down the hill inside the tunnel

so nobody would see them. They would take them out to the railroad cars and load them onto a railroad car or a person could pick them up down there. They were trying to be very respectful and trying to keep the patients that were alive, you know, kinda try to keep their spirits up and give them some sort of hope for survival. And yet they still had to respectfully had to get the remains of the patients that didn't survive to their homes.

They didn't want people to were in this hospital literally seeing people dying every hour. So what they would do is sneak them out through that tunnel down to the bottom and hearses would pick them up.

Both main roads that come up to the hospital, come up on the back side of the building. Which is very visible to all of the patients that would be in the Solarium. So the doctors came up with the idea of using that same tunnel to transport bodies out of the hospital so that the patients wouldn't see hearses coming up and lower their morale.

Douglas Steele: There was a reason for doing it and I think it's a plausible one.

Mr. Thornberry: There never was but one hearse that ever come up to this building. And the doctor claimed that it upset a patient, and they had this tunnel built right here. and they put that dead wagon right in there.

Sarah Gilbert: Just about everyone that came in that didn't survive you know, their remains went through this tunnel and when we went in there it was about 20 degrees cooler than it was outside and it was nighttime so it was very dark in there and it was just it was one of the spookiest places I have ever been in. You just had a different feeling when you went in there.

Kim Johnstone: It's almost as if you feel like there is someone behind you, like there is an energy behind you. Or there is something pulling you.

Last time we were here we recorded an EVP. What I did was; we walked down this 500 foot tunnel with tape recorder in hand and you could hear spectral breathing.

Jessica Mathis, one of assistants went down in the death tunnel and got some strange pictures. She actually caught one seems to be; a young boy with shorts, it is an incredible photo.

What happened was we were all down at the bottom of the tunnel, basically make storyboards for the shoot, I turned around and of course everybody just left me there. I guess I was a slow-poke or something and they left left me behind. I was like this is great, Ok, cool. Now I gotta walk up the tunnel by myself. Ah, no problem. So I turned around and started walking back up the tunnel and suddenly I don't know what it was, I just felt really ill, just like something really tragic happened and it was like a feeling, a gut feeling. And I just got in my head, I got to take a photo of this, so I took a photo and then I ran, all the way up out of the tunnel. Anyway, basically to make a long story short, we didn't think about it too much and then two weeks later, we sat down to go through the pictures I took in that tunnel, and there she was, a little girl standing in front of me with no eyes.

We were there to scout and write a script but we also needed to figure out budget and logistics. For example, how were we going to run generator cables down through this 500 foot body chute to power our lights? The only source of light in this claustrophobic hole was from the small underground air vents above.

Philip the Director, Marcel the DP (Director of Photography) and I the Producer in the Lead cautiously journeyed down this tunnel of death, every step being even scarier than the last. Of course it didn't help that all the hospital's history and ghost stories Keith told us about were stuck in my head.

Finally reaching the bottom of the death tunnel, I looked behind me only to see that my crew-mates, Philip and Marcel had disappeared. They must have headed back up to home base.

Suddenly a feeling of extreme dread took over, a feeling

of complete terror and desperation. Alone and now frightened, I felt like someone or something was standing right in front of me. I very much needed to get out of there and fast. I reached for my camera and snapped a picture and bolted up the dark tunnel with my video/audio recorder rolling. The run seemed endless as I was afraid to look back, scared that some monster may be chasing me.

Finally, I reached the top of the tunnel, out of breath, I collapsed and started to violently throw up. Something awful must have gone on down there, something very wicked indeed. I needed to figure out what the hell just happened. Hopefully I had caught something on my recorder.

Now back in Los Angeles. It was time to start production for this film. I loaded up the Waverly Hills scout pictures I had shot while on location and started the long process of reviewing them.

Suddenly that feeling of dread returned as I came across the picture I had taken at the bottom of the tunnel. The premonition of someone or something standing in front of me became quite clear. My photo revealed, a little girl. Emerging from the shadows, clear as day you could you could see her ghostly face, her long dark hair and her black, hollowed out eyes. What also is quite strange is, if you turn the photo upside down it is a perfect picture of three hooded figures in brown robes holding knives. Almost like a scene from a satanic ritual or sacrifice. One of the faces is clearly that of a high priestess and african american woman staring you right in your eyes. Freaky and shocking as it sent shivers down my spine bringing back the dark memory of that day inside the tunnel. Truly frightening, the little girl was like something out of a nightmare. Yet, I felt sorry for her as she projected feelings of sadness and loss. With a heavy heart I now dared to play the audio that was recorded that day in the death tunnel.

The sound of screaming, cries from a young female being violently attacked filled the room. I could not help but put my hands over my ears and try and make it stop. The pain of not being able to help ripped me apart. Not only did I capture this ghost girl's picture and voice but possibly her death as well.

You see it was the feeling of her presence, I experienced first that led me to take that picture and record sound. Needless to say this art heist film we initially set out to write a script for, changed drastically.

I remember saying, *"Lets tell the story of what really really happened. Here is the script idea. All the history and the ghost stories, the people breaking in and all the twisted-ness that went down. Let's make this movie about the real place."*

And at that time, Death Tunnel, the Sony Pictures film and the Syfy documentary Spooked - The Ghosts of Waverly Hills Sanatorium was born.

I had spent over three years researching, documenting the history and haunting of Waverly Hills Sanatorium. Many nights alone, surrounded only by cameras trying to find spirits to prove their existence. A touching interview with a previous staff member, Mr. Thornberry solidified the local legend of Room 502 and the Nurse's aborted baby.

"She made a mistake, got pregnant.... killed herself, they showed us where they found that baby."

An elderly couple who had contracted Tuberculosis told us they felt like second class citizens and were treated like lepers.

"I think that the initial draw of the place for most people is going to be the hauntings, and the legends and such. People are naturally curious about that. But, more and more it seems like people that go up there interested in the hauntings end up getting some kind of a respect for the history and the building itself."

-John Amerine, WHS Historian

"It is an urban legend in the Louisville area that this place is haunted. And I didn't believe that myself until I came up here,

and now I know its haunted."

- Charlie Mattingly, Waverly Hills Owner

"We don't know why these things do it, you can't explain why shadows, when all the sudden you hit them with a laser and the light doesn't go through them. Why you are even seeing a shadow in the first place and when it's coming at you the temperature drops 30 to 40 degrees." - Keith Age. Ghost Hunter

You just can't explain it, a lot of the things I have seen or heard or smelled up here, shadows, weird lights, you name it."

- Tina Mattingly, Waverly Hills Owner

"When the train come by, all these bodies from Kentucky come here, had to come here."

-Joe Mattingly, Waverly Hills Janitor

"A nurse, so depressed over the conditions of people dying up here from tuberculosis, took her own life by hanging herself."
Ronald Parkhurst, Waverly Hills Security

"He said, you saw her didn't you? And I went, How do you know? And she goes, You saw Mary, I said Yeah, She said well yeah, we heard her giggling this morning."

103

The Incurable: History and Haunting Of Waverly Hills Sanatorium

- Philip Booth, Death Tunnel Director

"All this stuff really happened in this place, I mean really, really happened. We went there to shoot a movie, but also got an amazing documentary out of it. By the interviews, the people, I mean yeah, its the passion of everybody, everybody that went there, I mean, the fact that we spent 14 hours in a 500 foot tunnel, I mean you just can't....you couldn't do that anywhere else and the fact that we got to go there and do this. I mean, it will never be done again" - Shane Taylor, Co-producer Death Tunnel

"You know, after seeing stuff I have seen up here, it does let me know that if anybody pisses me off I can come back and haunt the hell out of them." -John Harr, Waverly Hills Security

Some of the people interviewed, this would be their last interview as they have passed on since. My memories of these dear souls is nothing short of being honored to tell their story. We smiled, laughed and cried together. I flew all the way from Louisville, Kentucky to Los Angeles wearing the same cowboy boots I wore in the bloody death tunnel. I couldn't wait to tell this chilling story.

Within this exploration, we were able to validate the

history, address the local legends, put a face to Mary the little girl on the third floor and give remembrance to the brave souls of Waverly Hills Sanatorium. All they wanted was to find a cure and it was our hope through this story they are able to find some kind of closure. The trials and tribulations of these poor souls will always be the stars. They are a wonderful cast I will never forget.

.... God Bless

Ðedicated to all the lost souls, the Incurable,

of Waverly Hills Sanatorium.

WAVERLEY BULLETIN

In 2004 I had the pleasure to meet a sweet lady patient Martha that was in Waverly Hills Sanatorium from 1939-1942. She gave me her copy of the 1940 and the 1941 Waverly Hills Bulletin. This was the treasured local Waverly Hills Sanatorium's newspaper that was written by the doctors, staff and the patients themselves. They had the printing press on premises in the sanatorium and would print out a few hundred copies monthly or quarterly. Since basically all of Waverly were under some kind of quarantine, it made sense to have their inside world create their outside news. Inside this bulletin you will find personal poems, stories, names, dates and information. Find out everything that happened, floor to floor as you read first hand from the patients point of view from their actual writings below.

SPECIAL THANKS TO MARTHA ALLEN FOR THE
1940 AND 1941 WAVERLY BULLETIN.

OFFICIAL STAFF

Dr. Benjamin L. Brock,   Dr. Oscar O. Miller,
Medical Director Sanatorium   Medical Director Clinics

W. R. Livermore, Secretary & Business Manager

RESIDENT STAFF

Senior Resident Physicians   Senior Medical Intern

Dr. Ellis O. Coleman   Dr. Herbert Clay
Dr. A. D. Mullen
Dr. L. A. Taugher
Dr. T. A. Woodson

Dr. Lawrence Nehil, Thoracic Surgeon

Mrs. Attie Hansbrough,   Laboratory Technician
Gilbert O. Perry,   X-ray Technician
N. John Grillo,   Pharmacist

Mrs. Margaret B. Pusey,   Superintendent of Nurses
Mrs. Eula Lutch,   Nite Supervisor

SUPERVISORS

Mesdames Grace Lochner and Rena Parson; Misses Mary Hodges,
Alice Duvall and Jimmie Sharpe

Mrs. Margaret Laugh, Dietitian; Mrs. Anna Hollis, Matron;
Mrs. Charlotte Stoll, O. T. Director; Miss Margaret Nord,
House Mother at Nurse's Home; Mrs. Lucille Allmend, Libra-
rian; James Hollis, Laundry Manager, and R. S. McConnell,
Engineer.

COLORED HOSPITAL

Dr. O. L. Ballard,   Senior Resident Physician
Dr. J. B. Ball,   Junior Resident Physician
Mrs. Esther Barrons,   Supervisor

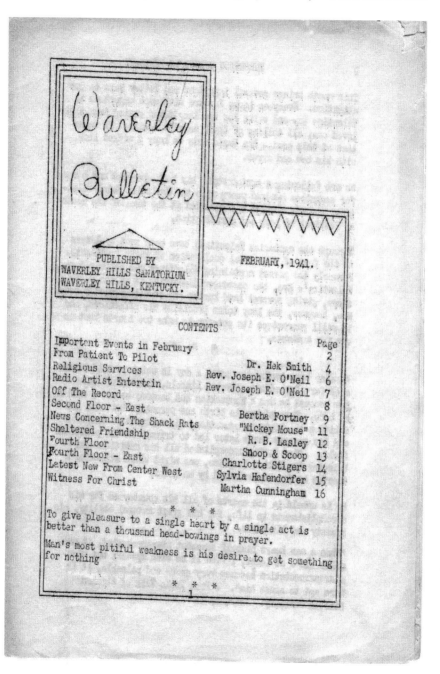

Waverley Bulletin

PUBLISHED BY
WAVERLEY HILLS SANATORIUM
WAVERLEY HILLS, KENTUCKY.

FEBRUARY, 1941.

CONTENTS

* * *

To give pleasure to a single heart by a single act is
better than a thousand head-bowings in prayer.

Man's most pitiful weakness is his desire to get something
for nothing

* * *

1

IMPORTANT EVENTS IN FEBRUARY

This month brings several important red letter days to our attention. Everyone looks forward with much eagerness to Valentine Day and waits for the lacy token coming from their loved one, all telling of their heart's desire. It seems that at this period Dan Cupid gets in many a wicked lick with his bow and arrow.

We are following a custom which has been observed and honored for seventeen hundred years when the Christian Saint Valentine, who was clubbed and beheaded at the time of the heathen festival of love and purification.

Through the centuries Valentines have been sent by lovers in the form of ornamental declaration of their sentiments. Formerly the parcel containing Valentines was delivered on Valentine's Eve, the messenger depositing it on the door-steps, giving several loud knocks and stealing quietly away. Now, however, the lacy token proclaims his affections, and it still guarantees its potency to make two hearts beat as one for a minute.

* * *

We also have during the month a day in which we hold reverence for a great man, Abraham Lincoln, whom we all know now because he was a Kentuckian but because he was a national hero. Born of humble birth and parentage but with the ambition to obtain an education, his ventures in business and his success there later led to triumph in the political field. After having accomplished all his ambitions and bringing the Nation to peace, one night while attending a theatre he was assassinated by an actor.

He is upheld in the hearts of all his countrymen for his accomplishments in life, for his great natural ability, his honesty and his humor.

"When a man hears himself somewhat misrepresented, it provokes him - at least, I find it so with myself; but when misrepresentation becomes very gross and palpable, it is more apt to amuse him". - From Table Talk of Abraham Lincoln Birthday - February 12

3

Are there any among us who do not remember the birthday of George Washington. If they do not remember that he was born on February 22nd, they will have heard the story of the lad who could not tell a lie about cutting down his father's cherry tree. We are not much concerned whether this story is true or not for it seems there are always stories like these told about our greatest heroes. It seems to stimulate the interest of little boys and girls when it is told to them and they want to know more about a naughty little boy something or so much like themselves.

Then when the story is told and one has unfolded the remarkable and useful history of his life, we read of a man, a Virginian, the first President of our land, known as the father of his Country and a citizen whom everyone loved, respected and admired.

Hasn't the story of the hatchet and the cherry tree served its purpose?

Genius is said to be an infinite capacity for taking pains. That definition of genius being true, we must regard Washington as a military genius. That he thought things but carefully, logically; that he had force, energy and ingenuity; daring when daring was necessary; caution when caution seemed wise, is evident from even a superficial study of the facts. But that which enabled him to endure and to triumph over all was his splendid character, which won the love of his soldiers and the confidence of his Country.

As we study him we are reminded that here was a great man with a great purpose, serving without compensation, moved by the one desire to help his fellowmen; one who could not be driven from his task by clumsy and intrigue, one who had marked out a line beyond which there could be no retreat; one who was mindful that his mission, as indeed the mission of every citizen of yesterday or today; should be expressed in the thought, citizenship and service go hand in hand.

* * *

Life cannot be made shockproof; man must be trained to "take it". Selected

4   FROM PATIENT TO PILOT

By Dr. Hek Smith
(National Tuberculosis Association)

By training, tradition and the tacit consent of the patient,
the doctor is a dictator - a benevolent dictator, thank God!
Fortunately, the really sick person wants to be bossed -
until the fever and the pain abate, when he begins again to
exercise his cantankerous democratic rights. ("You must
let me get up, doctor" — "No, I hate milk" etc.) But
absolute dictatorship does not work in the treatment of
tuberculosis. Here, we are dealing with a long-drawn-out
struggle, the outcome of which depends almost entirely
upon what the patient is willing to do for himself. The
patient's own conscience and understanding must guide his
course in the innumerable petty and critical situations
of daily life. He cannot be under the constant super-
vision of his doctor and one foolish act may undo the
gains purchased by months of expensive care.

The active case of tuberculosis is like a ship shattered
by stormy seas. He needs first and foremost, repairs.
That's why he is in the sanatorium. But what is going to
enable him to stand further stress after the actual damage
has been repaired. He can stand a few years in dry-dock
but to resign himself thereafter to a mill-pond existence
for the rest of his life is intolerable defeatism. There-
fore, the patient while getting well must, himself, learn
to command his own ship. Time and again he may have to
call upon his doctor for special piloting but in the end,
he is the captain in a voyage which lasts for life. It is
not enough that the sanatorium be a dry-dock, it must be a
training station for the patient.

The essence of the cure (for most cases at least) consists
in learning a new way of life. While the tubercle bacillus
is the sole, direct cause of the disease, environment (in
its broad sense) tips the scale in favor of, or against,
the infected person. Of the many people who are invaded by
bacillus tuberculosis, only those few whose mode of life or
environment or attitudes (again in a broad sense) violate

5

nature's demands, are most likely to develop the disease. And
if, after arrest of the disease has been achieved, the patient
returns to his old ways and attitudes, he may be inviting a
repetition of the disaster. That is why the modern sanatorium
tries to make a diagnosis of the patient's habits of living
and thought pattern. Mental attitude, perhaps, comes first
for hope, cheerfulness and confidence are the patient's staunch-
est allies, and depression of spirits his cruelest enemy.

However, cheerfulness that is put on like a top coat or like a
cosmetic will not outlast the grueling experience of the cure
with its many ups and downs. No, unless well-grounded in a
sound philosophy of life, hope is likely to give way to deeper
despair. Self-deception will not do. Indeed, for most patients
the best policy is to face frankly the fact that an unwelcome
guest has established headquarters in his lungs and that for the
rest of his life he must effect a truce with the invader, the
terms of which call upon the patient to surrender cherished desires for guarantee of bacterial peace. (And fortunately an arm-
istice with nature is more to be relied upon than a treaty with
one of the modern dictators.)

Understanding of the basic biological principles underlying
tuberculosis steers the patient in the right direction and gives
him the reasons for changing his attitudes. He should learn of
course why such scrupulous attention is paid to sputum disposal.
He should learn also the numerous ways in which tubercle bacilli
migrate from one person to another. He should develop automatic
habits of safety--something akin to the surgeon's "aseptic conscience." To learn by rote that kissing, spitting, the use of
common eating utensils, etc. are forbidden, is well, but not
enough. To know the general biology of the disease; the manner
in which the germ gets from one person to another, and how it
does its deadly work, is better. Give the average person an
understanding background and a few specific examples, and he
will, himself, regulate his conduct to the best interests of
others and his own good.

From an understanding of his own tuberculosis and the desire to
afoid infecting his loved ones and friends, is but a short step
to the cultivation of an interest in the larger problem of com-
continued on page 7

113

6   RELIGIOUS SERVICES

Rev. Joseph E. O'Neil

Be ye kind one to another, tenderhearted, forgiving one
another, even as God for Christ's sake hath forgiven you.
                              – Ephesians 4:32

              Breathe on us, Breath of God,
              'Till I am wholly Thine,
              'Till all this earthly part of me
              Glows with Thy fire divine.
              "Think God's thoughts after Him."

Patients at Waverley were not forgotten during the National
Christian Mission, which was conducted in the city during
January. On January 21, Mr. and Mrs. Philip Lee were in
charge of our midweek service. Mr. Lee is secretary of The
National Christian Broadcasting Company of China. They
brought messages which were an inspiration to our patients
and Mr. Lee, who has a beautiful voice, sang several special
numbers. This fine Chinese couple plan to return to their
native land, where they will carry on a Christian work among
their own people. We wish to thank Mr. Frank Gregg, Executive Secretary of the Louisville Council of Churches, through
whose kindness this service was made possible.

During January we had two midweek services which were deeply
appreciated by our patients. The first was on January 7, when
a group of young people from the Carlile Avenue Baptist
Church took charge and brought a most helpful program. On
the following Tuesday evening, this service was led by the
Rev. A. W. Walker, pastor of the Shively Baptist Church. The
Rev. Walker, who is a friend of the institution, is always a
welcome visitor and we do enjoy his inspirational messages.

We cordially invite every one to listen in on our Sunday
morning radio service. This service is broadcast at eight
o'clock.
                      *   *   *
The writers against religion, whilst they oppose every
system, are wisely careful never to set up any of their own.
                              – Selected

RADIO ARTISTS ENTERTAIN

One evening during our Christmas celebration, we were entertained by The Golden West Cowboys. This organization broadcasts regularly over radio station WHAS. After the show which was given in our auditorium, these artists broadcast a brief program over our microphone. This made it possible for patients who were unable to go to the auditorium, to enjoy the entertainment. This delightful evening was arranged for us by The Exchange Club of Louisville. Those attending the show were given a treat, provided by The Exchange Club. For several years, this Club has arranged a lovely Christmas party for our patients.

CATHOLICS GIVE TREAT

On Sunday morning, December 22, members of the St. Vincent de Paul Society came out and brought a treat of candy and fruit to all our patients. There were also gifts for our younger patients. The most popular visitor was Santa Claus. He visited all the floors and you may be sure he was given a hearty welcome. These friends never fail our patients at Christmas. They have been carrying on this splendid work for a long time.

NEW YEAR'S DAY

On New Year's Day, Open House was observed from nine in the morning until five o'clock in the afternoon. Then, too, there was a splendid dinner which was enjoyed by every one. During the afternoon, football fans listened to various bowl games which were broadcast. It was a happy day for all of us.

Continued from page 5
bating the pandemic, tuberculosis. Every patient who leaves the sanatorium should have in his mind a broad picture of tuberculosis as it affects the nation as a whole. The graduate of a sanatorium then becomes a crusader striking his blows in season and out of season. In him burns an everlasting fire. There are thousands like him. Against the cumulative effect of such force the old, old enemy is bound sooner or later to crumble.

8

OFF THE RECORD
with
APOLOGIES TO HARRY BLOOM

To all of Carolyn Pigg's intimate friends: Please stay away from her room at meal times. Since her last trip to the Dentist she is experiencing a little difficulty in eatin.

We are wondering if Thelma Bryan was trying to outdo the Original Early Bird Tuesday morning, when she got up at ten minutes of four to get to Church at six o'clock. It was her first time to go to Church after her recent promotion to the Main Dining Room and she was afraid that she would not awaken, so she asked one of the girls to call her early and the girls evidently wanted her to be the early bird and got the worm.

The reason for the puzzled expression on Napoleon Gilbert's face the past few days is, that he is trying to figure out why the "Middle Sized Bear" ran away from him the other morning. Ask us, we know.

Down in the center section there is lots of fun and laughter due to one of the new arrivals on the porch. Mrs. Babbitt's wit and humor keeps everybody laughing most of the time. It was hard to tell when she was having her history taken recently, just who was asking the questions and answering them.

Famous Last Words of one of the boys on the Third Floor - "Well, I guess I'll go down and go to bed." Be careful, Joe, and don't get offended if the boys buy you a shovel.

Maybe Walt Disney would like to have a drawing for his next picture of Sarah Johnson going to the Small Dining Room the other morning with her newest pet, "Mickey" (or was it Minnie) perched on her shoulders.

Skinny patient to Fat Patient as they meet at the Bathroom door- "Ha, Ha, it surely takes a lot of water for you to take a bath". Fat patient to Skinny one: "Ha, Ha, yourself, it doesn't take nearly as much water to fill the tub when I am in it as it does when you are in it."

Continued on next page

SECOND FLOOR - East
by
Bertha Fortney

How do you do it, Hazel? Let us in on it. By the way, Miss
Prewitt, **has** a friend who comes all the way from Detroit to
see her.

Since Bertha and Betty are in the dog house, their friends
have been very thoughtful to see that they won't starve.
They are receiving Miller's doggie dinner daily through the
mail. Good Luck! Hope your stay in the dog house won't be
long.

Annie don't think Hettie won't take a dare!!!!

Bob Hope, Yehudi has been found. Sarah Johnson knows where
he is.

Since Christmas, Elnore has been very "watchful" - if you
get what we mean.

Edna Crawford and Thelma are doing nicely with their jigsaws.

Carolyn Evans is having fun these days playing with dolls,
but to us she is "our" doll baby.

Mary Janes can't be beat when it comes to taking the cure -
just keep it up.

Carolyn Pigg has a shadow. The only place we don't see
Camden with her is in the dentist chair.

We are happy to welcome Mrs. Skaggs, Mrs. Lunch and Miss
Stratton to our Section.

Mrs. Collins, we miss you a lot and hope you'll soon be
back at the Main.

Continued on next page

Continued from page 8
Wilkins is about to wear out his RCA phonograph playing Glen
Miller's Records. He starts at five A. M., playing **"Five** O'clock
Whistle" and ends up at night playing, "Beat Me, Daddy, Eight To
The Bar". The boys are threatening to do a "Blitzkrieg" with
those records. Anyway, he **could** play a few Guy Lombardo Records,
which are his favorites.

SECOND FLOOR - East
                                      Continued

The girls in the Ward seem very happy these days. They are all
up and going places.

Mrs. Ewing, Mrs. Bryant and Lena Jones go to the Main and Mrs.
Parido and Mrs. Braden were promoted to Small Dining Room.

Oral Puckett, better be careful, Pigg's awful jealous of her
"Boy Friend". We have heard you are now on his list.

Eunice and Mrs. Walker, Lucille Scobie has fallen in love
with your music boxes. Wishes she had a boy friend to give
her one.

Mrs. Moore is doing fine these days.

A good cure for the blues - call on Mrs. Joyce and Mrs.
Childs in 219.

Jinny Hall is going to have to start jotting things down.
Looks like she can't depend on her roommate's memory any
more. She's got the "can't remembers".

THIRD FLOOR - East End Flasher

All the patients in the East End were sure glad to hear that
Aunt Kate Morgan so completely enjoyed Saturday's matinee of
Hellzapoppin.

One patient wishes to personally give another certain patient
in room 319 medical attention in the form of a rib operation.

All the patients join in wishing Dr. Taugher unlimited success
in his new post.

THIRD FLOOR - West

This Section boasts two father - son combinations: E. W.
Head and son, Joe, and Ira Flake and son, Ivan. Beat that,
if you can.

Last Saturday promotion day came leaving in its wake three
disappointed young men. Rumor has it they'll get what they
expected this week.

They say George Cooner sent his radio home last week.....
Complained he couldn't get anything except Highland Park.

NEWS CONCERNING THE SHACK RATS
11
by
"Mickey Mouse"

"Pony Boy" Callahan, the big commission man, is now singing,
"I Got Hosses, I Got Numbers On My Mind".

Howard (Butch, the Ripper) Jackson is quite pleased with the
rapid growth of his misplaced supercilium. Here's a secret,
Gals. He's definitely on the make.

Lasley, Harmon, Hill and Anderson are known as the hairless
pups.

Oscar (Arch Duke) Royalty is the Shack's most prominent Monogol-
ist. He's heard nightly fussing at Radio Announcers and singing
commercials. Good work, Oscar. Keep it up.

Pitellko, the Cop, wouldn't work on the Bulletin until someone
told him it was to be a "Police Gazette". Oh, Boy!

Why does money make Hammer's eyes turn green?

If anyone has something to invent, please communicate with
Raymond Gallahue.

Elmer (Junior) Nichter, the Boy with the "pimply puss" informs
me that he is in the market for a Dermatologist. Anybody got
one?

Jimmie (In Love) Morris is that way about a certain little
girl who comes to the Main. Hi, Sonia!

   The boys all want to know the name of the big,
beautiful "Blonde Lorelei" who just recently started to the
Main. Me too! Woo, Woo.
    ****

Overheard on the Highway between Waverley Hills and Louisville.
Highway Patrolman to lady he had just stopped for speeding:
"Where do you think you're going? You were making fifty-five
miles an hour back there."
"Lady Driver: "Why, Officer, I'm going to Waverley Hills to
get my husband. He hasn't been home for six months."
Highway Patrolman: "Lady, don't let me stand in your way,
get going."

12   SHELTERED FRIENDSHIP!

A little house, quaint with steeply sloping roof,
    A door that smiles a welcome, as it gently swaings a-jar,
A chimeny tall, with curling smoke stands proud, but not aloof,
    It coaxes you to enter, before you go afar.

Within its walls one finds a peace pervading,
    Each room is filled with laughter, like a child's happy
                                    heart.
A fragrant warmth affects one like a sweet voice pleading;
    As it foretells a reluctance to depart.

You glimpse a garden from yon window, hidden almost from view,
    It allures one to idle midst the flowers living there,
While it soothes the vexing doubts youth and age are due,
    Filling one with awe at nature's challenge unaware.

A little house, filled with every want that hungered of old,
    It infolds within its snuggness a trust that is true and
                                    fine,
It bestwos a lasting welcome, sincere, with a charm that is
                                    multifold.
    A happy little house holding a friendship that is
                                    yours and mine!
                    - By R. B. Lasley

_____

From a First Floor Snooper -
What recent biological catastrophe has happened to handsome
Charles "Playboy" Hardin to deflate that very pronounced
super ego of his "tsh tah". Pride goeth before a fall.

_____

It is of great interest to many of our old-timers to hear
from a former patient, Leona George Firestone. Mr. and Mrs.
C. D. Firestone, Canton, Ohio, announce the birth of a
daughter on January 10, 1941.

FOURTH FLOOR   13
by
Snoop & Scoop

In a remote spot on the Fourth Floor is the East Center Section.
There may be a few who do not know about us but a bit of snoop-
ing reveals the latest news.

Take Rita for instance. Thinking of her without her earphones
would seem as odd as thinking of Bergen without Charlie.

Mildred, having learned recently to crochet, is putting her
energy into a beautiful bedspread.

How "Bobbie" does look forward to Saturday afternoon and those
operas. And with such enthusiasm!!!!

> Mary found a little mouse
> Among her souvenirs.
> "Oh, Nursie! Come and take it out"
> Now, Mary, dry your tears.

Oh, Yes! Who is the little (?) lady who surely must enjoy her
siesta for she can be heard by the girls in the East.

We hear that Carrie is very much interested in a certain radio
announcer, having received a letter and a photograph.

Beulah, with your head tucked under the covers, we wonder if
you are dreaming of "Ole Virginny."

<u>Her Choice</u>
"What is the height of happiness?
"In my case he's about five feet, seven inches."

Virginia, you surely aren't tied to your mother's apron strings,
for you have plenty of your own. You've made some mighty
pretty ones.

I know "Jenny" Johnson had a sweet romance once even if she did
remain an old maid.

Ada, who is usually very quiet, goes on a rampage with a cross-
word puzzle when not "knitting tiny garments." Continued on next page

14
FOURTH FLOOR - East
by
Charlotte Stigers

What would we do without our smiling friend, Babe Deffrey? Whats' yo' heah for? Huh?

Iris is our baby and a nice one that never cries but stays in her own little bed without a whimper.

The Ward X is far in the lead with the most pounds, best disposition and sunniest outlook. The nickname for the group could be "The Optimistic Seven".

To the Surgery patients and those in private rooms, we send a cheery hello and our best wishes.

Anna Mae and Edna Lawrence are always present but seldom heard. They really are the best caretakers.

Dear Elizabeth and Bess, two pretty brunettes who can be found more oten under layers of blankets on the porch, reminding us of two little Eskimoes.

Wonder why Edna Mae Shipp named Walter Honeybear after Nell Smith's husband? Nell doesn't mind anyone thinking how handsome he is but Honeybear is just cute.

Attractive Rosa Coghill leads the East Section in the 1941 Style Show.

These are the titles of a few books now being read in the East: "Bess and the Cream" by Downs; "What's Yo' Heah For? by Deffrey; "Eat When You Are Hungry", by Edna Mae Shipp; "I'd Walk A Mile For An Onion", by Stigers.

Continued from page 13
There's a certain redhead here (no names mentioned) who surpasses Scarlette O'Hara by far. No wonder all the fellows flock around when she rolls those eyes.

Juanita, February 14th holds nothing for you as you no longer need Cupid. Considering all those letters, you are "on the last lap" now.

LATEST NEWS FROM CENTER WEST   15
by
Sylvia Hafendorfer

Well, here I am in the year 1941
Back to invite you readers to join in on the fun
We have added to our Roll Call about four or five
So, if you'll bear with me I'll now dish out
                    the five.

A blond haired miss about seventeen, not so very tall
Has joined us and is interested in a young man who's named Paul
Marjorie Kirby is her name and well, I'm tellin' you
It's Paul this and Paul that very other word or two.

Now another one we have with us is our friend called Opal Flake,
For adding her bit of knowledge she really takes the cake,
And let me add - there's one thing that makes her dance with joy
And that's when she sees someone who so name rhymes with boy.

Miss Ryan, Mrs. Tate and Mrs. Sullivan, we're glad to have you all
And hope ye 'll enjoy being on our Center West Roll Call
Here's wishing you a speedy recovery so that from day to day
You'll all feel stronger and stronger in every single way.

                That's all the news I have for you
                So guess I'll say adieu
                Until the next Bulletin when I'll
                    be seeing you.

_____

FOURTH FLOOR - West
by Yehoadi's M & M

Our loss was Third Floor's gain - We certainly miss Dr. Taugher
but hope to see him quite often.

We welcome our three new patients, Edna Jean Bryant, Mary Anderson and Evelyn Grisson. Hope their stay is short and sweet.

Our two Vogue stylists, Ellie Reed and Margaret Thompson, are
Continued on next page

16   WITNESS FOR CHRIST
                           Romans 1:16

Oh, speak a word for Jesus,
    Wherever you may be;
He has no other witnesses,
    But saved ones such as we.

Then let us never fail Him,
    But gladly day by day,
Pass on the invitation
    To those on Life's highway.

So many are faint-hearted
    And need a cheering word;
The tender tone of sympathy
    May draw them to the Lord.

We have the only Gospel
    That sets the captive free,
That paints men to their Saviour
    Who died on Calvary.

Then tell it out, rejoicing,
    That men may hear and know
How Jesus died to save them,
    Because He loved them so.
                    - Marion Murray
            Submitted by Martha Cunningham,
                        Fifth Floor - West

                    *   *   *.

Continued from page 15
setting examples for the latest Spring styles at the Main

Rachel Garvin has decided it's O.K. with her for Viginia to
marry Lloyd, as she has decided she kinder likes him. But
they really aren't married, you know!

The every day 3 o'clock thrill! That's the time Portio comes
on and the three constant listeners are Sue Carter, Cora Lee
Campbell and Boss Pearl. You'd think they were discussing
real life to hear them talk about Portio facing life.

If Rosie Page isn't more careful about talking in her sleep at
night, we'll be finding out just who is her secret admirer! Beware!

Our two newest curley tops are Mary Williams and Roberta Payton.
Just who are they fixing up for?

Lizzie Wessel certainly wears a big smile these days. And no wonder
With a son going places in the business world.

INTERVIEW CREDITS & THANKS

TO THE CAST AND CREW OF

SPOOKED
THE GHOSTS OF WAVERLY HILLS
SANATORIUM

A BOOTH BROTHERS FILM

SPECIAL THANKS

GOD

Keith Age

Sean Penn

Philip Adrian Booth

Rachel Marie Booth

Alyss and Gabriel

SPOOKED PRODUCTIONS &
TWINTALK ENTERTAINMENT
presents

a BOOTH BROTHERS film

SPOOKED
THE GHOSTS OF WAVERLY HILLS SANATORIUM

Produced and Directed by
CHRISTOPHER SAINT BOOTH

Written by
PHILIP ADRIAN BOOTH
CHRISTOPHER SAINT BOOTH

INTERVIEWS

CHARLIE MATTINGLY
Waverly Hills owner

TINA MATTINGLY
Waverly Hills Historical Society

JOE MATTINGLY
Waverly Hills Employee

KEITH AGE
Louisville Ghost Hunters Society

R. THORNBERRY
Waverly Hills Worker

CATHY L. GALES
WoodHaven Nurse

RON PARKHURST
Waverly Hills Historian & Security

ROY MUIR
Waverly Hills Memorial & Historical Resource

BIG JOHN HARR
Waverly Hills Security

ALECIA WALTERS
Waverly Hills Security

TOM SWARTZ
Waverly Hills Security

SARAH GILBERT

Waverly Hills Historian

CHRIS HABERMAN
Fangoria Magazine Journalist

DOUGLAS T. STEELE
Waverly Hills Patient

MARY R. STEELE
Waverly Hills Patient

DELORES WEBSTER
Waverly Hills Patient

CHARLES WEBSTER
Waverly Hills Patient

JOHN AMERINE
Waverly Hills Historian

PHILIP BOOTH
Death Tunnel Director

CHRISTOPHER SAINT BOOTH
Death Tunnel Producer

Waverly Hills Locals
KIMBERLY JOHNSTONE
MONICA PAYNE
ANDREA THOMPSON

Interviewer
ARIANNE FRAZER

INSCURSON 502
Jeremy Robertson
Nick Houpt
Brian Hart
Tim Holder
Erik Angelini
Van Avery

GHOST HUNTERS
Kenneth S. Gales Jr.
Jessica Lynn Morris
Julie McGrath
Cathy Flecher
Sean Penn
Missy Vixxy Baughn
Jessica Lynn Mathis
Shelly Gibson
Lauren Gassman
James H. Lowry
Jeff Hawkins
Laura Corum

DT INTERVIEWS
Steffany Huckaby
Annie Burgstede
Melanie Lewis

University of Louisville Students
Kristen Novak
Yolanda Pecoraro

Location Manager
CHARLIE & TINA MATTINGLY

Waverly Hills Research Consultants
RONALD PARKHURST
CHARLIE & TINA MATTINGLY
KEITH AGE
CHRISTOPHER SAINT BOOTH
JOHN AMERINE

Additional research
Louisville Ghost Hunters Society,
International Ghost Hunters Society, Prairie Ghosts
Waverly Hills Memorial Society, University of Louisville, Courier Journal,

The Incurable: History and Haunting Of Waverly Hills Sanatorium

American Tuberculosis Association

ROY MUIR & PAM BROOKS
http://whsmemorial.tripod.com

Film Footage
RICK PRELINGER-ARCHIVE.ORG
Creative Commons - Public Domain

On The Firing Line - Courier Productions, Inc
© Creative Commons

City Of Hope 0572 PA8041© Creative Commons

Murder Mills 1945/04/26 © Creative Commons

Forty Years Of Human Service0572 PA8042
© Creative Commons

Mental Hospital- University Of Oklahoma
© Creative Commons

Tuberculosis (Third Edition) Encyclopedia Britannica Film
© Creative Commons

Legal Services
ROBERT JOHNSON, ESQ

SPOOKED ORIGNAL SOUNDTRACK
BY CHRISTOPHER SAINT
AVAILABLE ON iTUNES and AMAZON

Special Thanks
WAVERLY HILLS SOCIETY
TEXAS ROADHOUSE
RED BULL
UNIVERSITY OF LOUISVILLE

MAKERS MARK
OLDHAM POLICE DEPARTMENT
SYFY CHANNEL
RAY CANELLA
CATHY GALES
ROY MUIR
CHARLIE & TINA

Documented On Location
WAVERLY HILL SANATORIUM
LOUISVILLE, KENTUCKY

WHS BLUE PRINTS are solely owned by their original artists.

Waverly Hills pictures are public domain.

DEATH TUNNEL IS LICENSED TO SONY PICTURES HOME
ENTERTAINMENT.

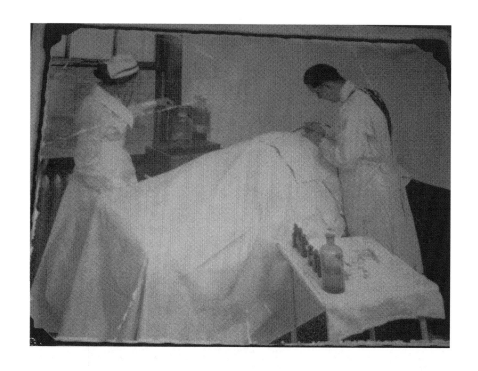

OTHER SPOOKED TV BOOK
SERIES VOLUMES COMING SOON

CHILDREN OF THE GRAVE
THE POSSESSED
THE EXORCIST FILE-HAUNTED BOY
CHILDREN OF THE GRAVE 2
SOUL CATCHER

ABOUT THE AUTHOR

Christopher Saint Booth born in Yorkshire, England started his career at an early age. Influenced by The Beatles, singing and strumming at the age of four. Atlantic crossing brought them to Canada where at the age of thirteen he were writing and performing at the local establishments. In 1978 he was invited to combine forces with, Juno award winner, Sweeney Todd. (London Records) Worldwide touring commenced immediately as their new gold album paved his way to sunny California. Upon arriving in Los Angeles, greeted with a publishing deal (RCA Music) he began writing vocalizations and musical scores for film, cable and television.

Desires of new creative outlets began development, now reaching out to the visual side of entertainment. Audio with Video studios were soon built to quench this creative thirst. Christopher, a successful film and music Director, Producer, Production Designer and Composer has written, edited, animated, directed and scored some of Billboard's Top Ten releases including, Film Features, Erotic Thrillers, Music Videos and worldwide releases.

Internationally renowned for his provocative style,Independent films soon broadened the horizon. Financing a million-dollar HD digital domain in Los Angeles California, this is where he would design and build his ultimate dreams. As well as endorsed by an array of electronic arts manufacturers, no boundaries would be left untouched. For every new technical toy that the eyes and ears could ever dream of soon became vivid. As an Apple licensed developer and 3rd party designer for SoftImage, AMP, APDA and Microsoft, Booth continued to design the future of entertainment and media for all platforms. New concepts with slick designs go hand in hand with the latest web technology

With over 100 features behind him built all from scratch

with the insight of what's happening tomorrow for the people today. A panoramic view of freedom with the fresh scent of change inspires this Saint to create a brave new world for your eyes and ears. Christopher is married to Rachel Marie and the father to Gabriel & Alyss B.

Christopher is an Author, Producer and Director of films and documentaries for Syfy, Chiller, NBC Universal, Spooked TV Productions, At&t, Vimeo, Apple iTunes, Netflix, Roku, Discovery and more worldwide. CEO of Spooked Television Releasing.

Films include Dead Still (Syfy), Death Tunnel (Sony Pictures), The Possessed, Spooked, Children Of The Grave (Syfy Channel/NBC Universal), The Exorcist File-Haunted Boy (Redbox), Children Of The Grave 2, Soul Catcher and DarkPlace. For sales more info: www.spookedtv.com

Christopher Saint Booth
Official-Site:www.christophersaintbooth.com
FaceBook:www.facebook.com/christophersaintbooth
Twitter: www.witter.com/sainttweets

OTHER BOOKS BY

CHRISTOPHER SAINT BOOTH

PARANOIA THE STRANGE CASE OF GHOSTS, DEMONS AND ALIENS

Journey beyond the screams with filmmaker Christopher Saint Booth as seen on Syfy, Chiller and Sony Pictures. Uncover the real stories behind the history and haunting of the Booth Brothers scariest films, cases and locations including Death Tunnel, Spooked The Ghosts Of Waverly Hills Sanatorium, Children Of The Grave, The Possessed and The Exorcist File. In this human emotional search for the afterlife, explore supernatural evidence, theories and techniques from the leading paranormal investigators, sensitives and demonologists.

www.paranoia.book.com

ISBN-13: 978-0692488904

THE EXORCIST DIARY

What intrigued me about this diary was that "The Exorcist" was by far the scariest horror movies of all time based on true events. The actual case involved a boy not a girl as portrayed in the movie. We went to St. Louis to find out the truth and uncover the real diary and we did just that. Documented by 14 priests this diary chronicles the horrific story of "The Exorcist" and a boy possessed by the devil. For the first time read the unedited diary of the boy's possession and exorcism. Learn the facts and truth about one of the most darkest supernatural cases known to man.

www.theexorcistdiary.com

ISBN-13: 978-0692536698

Also available on Amazon, Barnes and Noble

and at www.spookedtv.com

ANGEL OR DEVIL

A dark historical adventure into the real journals of America's first documented Possessions and Exorcisms. Unedited and presented as evidence, these emotional case files reveal the truth and prove the supernatural realm does indeed exist in our sacred world.

Case files explore in depth and accuracy the first documented Erling, Iowa Exorcism: A legion of demons inhabit a young girl in 1928. Brought to a convent for an exorcism, disturbing and extraordinary events lash out due to the families dark magic that creates a stronger than evil curse.

Witness the Watseka Wonder: America's first documented possession of 1877. A chilling story of a 13-year-old girl from the small town of Watseka, Illinois who became possessed or reincarnated by spirits of the insane dead.

Some called them Angels, others called them Devils, they all were branded, POSSESSED!

www.angelordevilbook.com

ISBN-13: 978-0692663646

Also available on Amazon, Barnes and Noble and at

WWW.SPOOKEDTV.COM

SPOOKED TV
FEATURE FILMS, DOCUMENTARIES, MUSIC AND BOOKS

www.spookedtv.com

VIDEO ON DEMAND

SPOOKEDtv-OD

www.spookedtv-od.com

Movies streaming on

AMAZON INSTANT VIDEO

The Incurable: History and Haunting Of Waverly Hills Sanatorium

(search Booth Brothers)

www.amazon.com

ORIGINAL SOUNDTRACKS

Amazon and iTunes

www.itunes.apple.com/us/artist/christopher-saint/id211036282

www.cdbaby.com/Artist/ChristopherSaint1

PARANOIA AUDIO BOOK EXPERIENCE

https://itunes.apple.com/us/album/paranoia-audio-experience/id1079060031

http://www.cdbaby.com/cd/christophersaintbooth2

Publishing House

SPOOKED TV PUBLICATIONS

18017 CHATSWORTH STREET #130

GRANADA HILLS, CA 91344

Email:

info@spookedproductions.com

Phone: 310-498-9576

VISIT US ON FACEBOOK

www.facebook.com/SPOOKEDtv

The Incurable: History and Haunting Of Waverly Hills Sanatorium

www.facebook.com/christophersaintbooth

TWITTER

www.twitter.com/spookedtv

OFFICIAL SITE

WWW.SPOOKEDTV.COM

INTRODUCTIONS

WRITTEN BY CHRISTOPHER SAINT BOOTH FROM

PARANOIA The Strange Case Of Ghosts, Demons and Aliens and THE

EXORCIST DIARY

PARANOIA The Strange Case Of Ghosts, Demons and Aliens

©2015 Spooked Productions

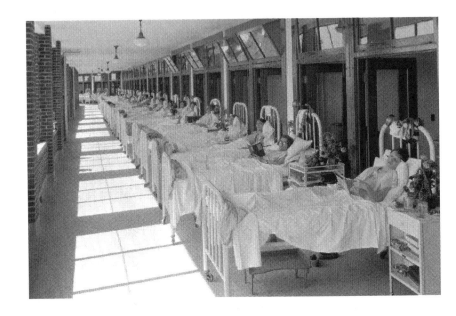

Dedicated to all the brave

patients of Waverly Hills Sanatorium

Woodhaven Geriatric Center.

Made in the USA
San Bernardino, CA
23 May 2016